INTERACTIVE

THE
BONDAGE
BREAKER®

NEIL T. ANDERSON

HARVEST HOUSE PUBLISHERS

EUGENE, OREGON

Cover by Dugan Design Group, Bloomington, Minnesota

THE BONDAGE BREAKER is a registered trademark of The Hawkins Children's LLC. Harvest House Publishers, Inc., is the exclusive licensee of the federally registered trademark THE BONDAGE BREAKER.

THE BONDAGE BREAKER® INTERACTIVE WORKBOOK
Copyright © 2011 by Neil T. Anderson
Published by Harvest House Publishers
Eugene, Oregon 97402
www.harvesthousepublishers.com

ISBN 978-0-7369-4538-7 (pbk.)

ISBN 978-0-7369-4539-4 (eBook)

Printed in the United States of America

11 12 13 14 15 16 17 18 19 / VP-SK / 10 9 8 7 6 5 4 3 2 1

CONTENTS

INTRODUCTION

Have you ever wondered why the church is so divided? Why marriages are failing? Why so many Christians continue to struggle in their faith even though they are forgiven and are new creations in Christ? I asked myself those questions many years ago when I was the pastor of a church. I believed that Christ is the answer and that truth sets people free, but I didn't see very many believers fully realize that freedom. I saw a lot of people come to Christ in those early years of ministry, but most continued to struggle with the same old issues. Where was the freedom that Christ promised?

When I was extended a call to teach on the faculty at Talbot School of Theology, I accepted with that burden. I offered an elective class on resolving personal and spiritual conflicts that grew numerically every year, and I started to learn how Christ sets captives free and heals our wounds. In the process I personally experienced several paradigm shifts. I discovered myself what it really meant to be a child of God and to be alive in Christ. I slowly discovered that every defeated Christian who came to me for help didn't know who he or she was in Christ. That is still true today.

The next major shift in my thinking had to do with the way we help others find their identity and freedom in Christ. To accomplish that requires a holistic approach that takes into consideration the reality of the spiritual world. The apostle Paul wrote, "The Spirit clearly says that in later times some will abandon the faith and follow deceiving spirits and things taught by demons" (1 Timothy 4:1 NIV). That is presently happening all over the world. Many Christians are struggling with tempting, accusing, and blasphemous thoughts. When you are established as alive and free in Christ through genuine repentance and faith in God, you will discover that "the peace of God, which transcends all understanding, will guard your hearts and your minds in Christ Jesus" (Philippians 4:7 NIV).

In the first six lessons I will share the whole gospel and explain the believer's identity in Christ. We will explore the battle for our minds and how we can have emotional freedom by forgiving others. After the first six lessons, you may choose to jump to lesson 13 and work through the Steps to Freedom in Christ. The Steps to Freedom provide a way for you to resolve personal and spiritual conflicts through genuine repentance and faith in God. They are means by which you personally connect with God, who is the only one who can set you free and heal your wounds from the past. The process will not embarrass you, and there is nothing to fear. The purpose is to set you free in Christ.

The recommended format is to go through all 12 lessons and then the Steps to Freedom. Lessons 7 through 12 focus on the believer's position, authority, and protection in Christ. I will share ways in which we are vulnerable and demonstrate how we can help others find their freedom in Christ.

Several exploratory studies have shown promising results regarding the effectiveness of the Steps to Freedom. Three studies were performed on participants who attended a conference similar to this video series. The first study involved 30 people, the second study involved 55 people, and the third study involved 21 people. The participants began by taking a questionnaire that assessed for levels of depression, anxiety, inner conflict, tormenting thoughts, and addictive behaviors. Then, as part of the conference, they were led through the Steps to Freedom. Three months later, they took the questionnaire again. The following table illustrates the percentage of improvement for each category.

	Study 1	Study 2	Study 3
Depression	64%	47%	52%
Anxiety	58%	44%	47%
Inner conflict	63%	51%	48%
Tormenting thoughts	82%	58%	57%
Addictive behavior	52%	43%	39%

Research was also conducted in Oklahoma City, Oklahoma, and Tyler, Texas, by a ministerial team chaired by Dr. George Hurst, who previously directed the University of Texas Health Center at Tyler. This study was in cooperation with a doctoral student at Regent University under the supervision of Dr. Fernando Garzon. The data were combined in a manuscript that was accepted by the Southern Medical Journal for publication.

Most people attending a video series like this one can work through the repentance process on their own using the Steps to Freedom. In our experience, about 15 percent can't because of difficulties they have experienced. A personal session was offered each of these participants with a trained encourager. They were given a pretest before a Steps to Freedom session and a posttest three months later. The following results show the percentage of improvement:

	Oklahoma City	Tyler
Depression	44%	52%
Anxiety	45%	44%
Fear	48%	49%
Anger	36%	55%
Tormenting thoughts	51%	27%
Negative habits	48%	43%
Sense of self-worth	52%	40%

I hope this research encourages you to take this course seriously. Does God want all His children to be free in Christ? Yes! "It was for freedom that Christ set us free; therefore keep standing firm and do not be subject again to a yoke of slavery" (Galatians 5:1 NASB). The truth will set you free, and Jesus is the truth as well as the Wonderful Counselor. My prayer is that you will finish this course with a sense of peace and freedom that only Christ can bring.

Dr. Neil T. Anderson

Part 1

THE GOSPEL
AND THE BELIEVER'S
IDENTITY IN CHRIST

CREATION IN CONFLICT

*God created man in his own image, in the image of God
he created him; male and female he created them.*

GENESIS 1:27

LESSON OBJECTIVE

To understand the creation account, the Fall, and the full meaning of
the gospel in order to have a clear perspective of the world in which we
live and how we can overcome it.

The Original Creation and the First Adam

To understand the problems that we have, we need to go back to the beginning. "The LORD
God formed man of dust from the ground, and breathed into his nostrils the breath of life; and
man became a living being" (Genesis 2:7 NASB). Adam experienced two kinds of life, and we do too:

- *Physical life* (Greek: *bios*). Our soul/spirit is in union with our body. To die physically
  is to separate the soul/spirit from the body.

- *Spiritual life* (Greek: *zoë*). Our soul/spirit is in union with God. To be spiritually
  dead is to be separated from God (Ephesians 2:1).

Before the Fall, mankind enjoyed...

- *Significance* (Genesis 1:28). Humanity had a divine purpose.

- *Safety and security* (Genesis 1:29-30). God provided for all of humanity's needs.

- *Belonging* (Genesis 2:18). Humanity had a sense of identity and belonging to God
  and each other.

The Effects of the Fall (Genesis 3:8–4:9)

"You shall surely die" (Genesis 2:17). When Eve was deceived and Adam deliberately chose to sin, they immediately died spiritually—they were separated from God. (Physical death was another consequence, but that came later.) The essence of Adam's fall was the deliberate breaking of his intimate relationship with God. Sin can be understood only in terms of our relationship to God and His will. Sinful behavior is the result of fallen humanity attempting to find purpose and meaning in life independent of God. We simply can't meet our own needs without the life of Christ.

As a result of the Fall, we are all born dead in our trespasses and sins.

- "Sin entered the world through one man, and death through sin" (Romans 5:12 NIV).

- "You were dead in the trespasses and sins in which you once walked, following the course of this world, following the prince of the power of the air, the spirit that is now at work in the sons of disobedience" (Ephesians 2:1-2). .

The Fall affected humanity in several ways:

1. *In our minds.* The concept of "knowing" was no longer relational (see Ephesians 4:17-18).

2. *In our emotions.* Humanity experienced...

   - fear and anxiety (Genesis 3:10)

   - shame and guilt

   - depression and anger (Genesis 4:5-6)

3. *In our wills.* Humanity has the wonderful power to make choices, but since the Fall, people have become inundated with opportunities to make poor choices.

4. *In our relationships.* Humanity had a sense of rejection and a need for belonging.

5. *In our guilt and shame.* People need acceptance and affirmation.

6. *In our weakness and helplessness.* People need strength and self-control.

To reestablish fallen humanity, Jesus came to...

- show us how to live

- die for our sins and give us life

- destroy the works of the devil

DISCUSSION QUESTIONS

1. What is the difference between natural life and spiritual life?

2. What attributes did Adam and Eve have as a result of creation that turned into needs as a result of the Fall?

3. What did Adam and Eve lose in the Fall, and how does that affect us today?

4. The serpent said, "Did God actually say, 'You shall not eat of *any* tree in the garden?'" (Genesis 3:1). What is wrong with the question, and what characteristic of God is the serpent questioning?

5. Eve said, "You shall not eat of the fruit of the tree that is in the midst of the garden, neither shall you touch it, lest you die" (verse 3). What did Eve add to God's command?

6. The serpent said, "You will not surely die" (verse 4). What characteristic of God is the serpent questioning?

7. Verse 6 reads, "So when the woman saw that the tree was good for food, and that it was a delight to the eyes, and that the tree was to be desired to make one wise, she took of its fruit and ate." What correlation do you see between those channels of temptation and this New Testament verse? "For all that is in the world, the lust of the flesh and the lust of the eyes and the boastful pride of life, is not from the Father, but is from the world" (1 John 2:16 NASB).

8. Satan used those same three channels to tempt Jesus (Matthew 4:1-11). How does knowing that help us today?

9. What one thing caused the change in Adam and Eve's mental and emotional state in Genesis 3? What conclusions can you draw from that?

10. What three objectives must God accomplish in order to reestablish fallen humanity?

2

IDENTITY IN CHRIST

The reason the Son of God appeared
was to destroy the works of the devil.

1 JOHN 3:8

LESSON OBJECTIVE

To understand the whole gospel in order to appreciate who we are and how God intends for us to live.

What Jesus Came to Do

Jesus came to die for our sins so we could go to heaven. That's true, but the gospel is much bigger than just that. The eternal life Jesus came to give us begins now!

1. Jesus showed us how a spiritually alive person can live and not sin (John 13:15; 1 Peter 2:21) that we might follow His example. How did Jesus live that way? By depending on the Father. Everything He spoke and did—His entire life—came from His Father. All temptation is an attempt to get us to live independently of God.

- "In him was life, and the life was the light of men" (John 1:4).

- "I can do nothing on my own" (John 5:30).

- "I came not of my own accord, but he sent me" (John 8:42).

- "The words that I say to you I do not speak on my own authority, but the Father who dwells in me does his works" (John 14:10).

- "Now they know that everything you have given me comes from you" (John 17:7 NIV).

2. Jesus came to die for our sins and give us life. If you wanted to save a dead man, you would have to do two things:

- Cure the disease that caused him to die (Romans 6:23a).

- Give him life (Romans 6:23b). The apostle Paul said, "For to me to live is Christ" (Philippians 1:21). Spiritual life is recovered in Christ. For the Christian to be spiritually alive is to be "in Christ" or "born again."

3. Jesus came to destroy the works of the devil (1 John 3:8).

The apostle Paul summarizes these three aspects of the gospel in Colossians 2:13-15:

> And you, who were dead in your trespasses and the uncircumcision of your flesh, God made alive together with him, having forgiven us all our trespasses, by canceling the record of debt that stood against us with its legal demands. This he set aside, nailing it to the cross. He disarmed the rulers and authorities and put them to open shame, by triumphing over them in him.

Who We Are in Christ

A Christian is not simply a person who gets forgiveness, who gets to go to heaven, who gets the Holy Spirit, or who gets a new nature. Being a Christian is not just getting something; it is being someone. People cannot consistently behave in a way that is inconsistent with what they believe about themselves. Salvation is transformation.

- We are children of God the moment we receive Him (John 1:12).

- We are purified by the hope of knowing who we are in Christ (1 John 3:1-3).

- There are no cultural, social, religious, racial, or sexual barriers for those who are in Christ (Galatians 3:24-28; 4:6; Colossians 3:11).

In Christ I Am Accepted

I am God's child (John 1:12).
I am Jesus' chosen friend (John 15:15).
I have been justified (forgiven) by faith and have peace with God (Romans 5:1).
I am united with the Lord and one with Him in spirit (1 Corinthians 6:17).
I have been bought with a price—I belong to God (1 Corinthians 6:20).
I am a member of Christ's body, a part of His family (1 Corinthians 12:27).

I am a saint, a holy one (Ephesians 1:1).

I have been adopted as God's child (Ephesians 1:5).

I have direct access to God through the Holy Spirit (Ephesians 2:18).

I have been bought back (redeemed) and forgiven of all my sins (Colossians 1:14).

I am complete in Christ (Colossians 2:10).

In Christ I Am Secure

I am free from condemnation (Romans 8:1-2).

I am assured that all things work together for good (Romans 8:28).

I am free from any condemning charges against me (Romans 8:31-34).

I cannot be separated from the love of God (Romans 8:35-39).

I have been established, anointed, and sealed by God (2 Corinthians 1:21-22).

I am hidden with Christ in God (Colossians 3:3).

I am sure God will finish the good work He has started in me (Philippians 1:6).

I am a citizen of heaven (Philippians 3:20).

I have not been given a spirit of fear, but of power, love, and a sound mind (2 Timothy 1:7).

I can find grace and mercy in time of need (Hebrews 4:16).

I am born of God, and the evil one cannot touch me (1 John 5:18).

In Christ I Am Significant

I am like salt and light for everyone around me (Matthew 5:13-16).

I am connected to the true vine, joined to Christ, and able to produce much fruit (John 15:1-5).

I have been chosen by Jesus to bear fruit (John 15:16).

I am a personal witness of Christ's life within me (Acts 1:8).

I am God's temple, where the Holy Spirit lives (1 Corinthians 3:16).

I am at peace with God, and He has given me the work of making peace between Himself and other people. I am a minister of reconciliation (2 Corinthians 5:16-21).

I am God's coworker (2 Corinthians 6:1).

I am seated with Christ in the heavenlies (Ephesians 2:6).

I am God's workmanship (Ephesians 2:10).

I may approach God with freedom and confidence (Ephesians 3:12).

I can do all things through Christ who strengthens me (Philippians 4:13).

All these verses are true about you if you have made the decision to trust in God and have received Him into your life. "For by grace you have been saved through faith. And this is not your own doing; it is the gift of God, not a result of works so that no one may boast" (Ephesians

2:8-9). If you have never made that decision, none of the statements in the lists above are true about you. If you have never received Christ, you can do so right now. God knows the thoughts and intentions of your heart, so all you have to do is put your trust in God alone. You can express your decision in a prayer like this one:

PRAYER

> Dear heavenly Father, thank You for sending Jesus to die on the cross for my sins. I acknowledge that I have sinned and that I cannot save myself. I believe that Jesus came to give me life, and by faith I now choose to receive You into my life as my Lord and Savior. By the power of Your indwelling presence, enable me to be the person You created me to be. I pray that You would grant me repentance leading to a knowledge of the truth so I can experience my freedom in Christ and be transformed by the renewing of my mind. In Jesus' precious name I pray. Amen.

DISCUSSION QUESTIONS

1. What kind of life did Jesus model for us?

2. Where do most people get their identity from?

3. How do most people perceive themselves? Why?

4. How important is it that we see ourselves the way God sees us?

5. What three things did Jesus come to do?

6. If we see only the cross and not the resurrection, how will that affect the way we live?

7. Why is knowing who we are in Christ so important?

8. Who is the ruler of this world? (See John 14:30; 16:10-11.)

9. What does Jesus hope to gain by undoing the works of the devil, and how should that impact us?

10. Summarize the gospel using Colossians 2:13-15.

3

MENTAL STRONGHOLDS

The weapons of our warfare are not of the flesh but have divine power to destroy strongholds. We destroy arguments and every lofty opinion raised against the knowledge of God, and take every thought captive to obey Christ.

2 CORINTHIANS 10:4-5

LESSON OBJECTIVE

To understand how conforming to this world develops strongholds in our minds, resulting in less than Christlike temperaments, so that we can begin the process of renewing our minds and become the people God created us to be.

We Are New Creations, yet We Struggle

When we are born again, God transfers us out of the kingdom of darkness and into the kingdom of His beloved Son. We are not in Adam; we are in Christ. We are new creations.

But because we were spiritually separated from God when we were physically born, we learned to live independently from Him. Though we become new creations when we are born again, our minds are still conformed to the world. The process of being transformed into the image of God takes time.

Why do we who are in Christ continue to struggle? How are strongholds raised up against the knowledge of God?

Stimulation

As we grew up, we assimilated the attitudes of our home, school, friends, church, and so on. We learned these attitudes primarily through two kinds of experiences.

- Prevailing experiences—the things we hear and see every day.

- Traumatic experiences, such as death in the family, abuse, divorce, and so on. People are not in bondage to past traumas. They are in bondage to the lies they believe because of the trauma.

Temptation

Temptation coerces us to live independently of God without consideration of the consequences. To be tempted is not a sin, and God has provided a way of escape (1 Corinthians 10:13). Temptation begins with thoughts that we must learn to take captive in obedience to Christ. Failure to do so will set off a chain of physiological events.

The outer self (the physical body) and the inner self (the soul) correlate together and function much like a computer operation, which has two distinct components—the hardware and the software. The brain is like the hardware, and the mind is like the software. Obviously, one can have a hardware problem, but the major emphasis in Scripture is directed toward the software—the mind.

The brain controls two peripheral nervous systems. The *somatic* nervous system regulates muscular movements, and that correlates with our will. The *autonomic* nervous system regulates all the glands, which we don't have direct volitional control over, and that correlates with our emotions. Emotions are primarily a product of our thought life, which we can control.

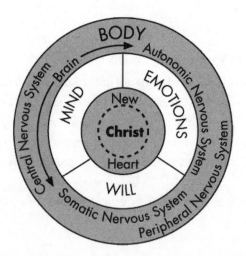

The Israelites saw the giant and heard his boasting. Those signals were sent to the brain, the mind interpreted the data, and that is what regulated the glands, resulting in an adrenaline rush.

They were fearful and anxious because of what they thought and believed. David interpreted the data differently because he saw the giant in relationship to God while the others saw the giant in relationship to themselves. David had faith in God because he had previously seen God deliver him from a lion and a bear. David's adrenal glands reacted differently from the other Israelites' because of what he chose to believe, not because he had better adrenal glands.

The brain cannot function any way other than how it has been programmed. We all experience stressful situations and sexual temptations, but the adrenal glands and sex glands are not the problem. We are not shaped by the environment, but by our perception of the environment—that is, by what we believe about the experiences of life. Life events do not determine our emotional response. How we mentally interpret life events determines our emotional response.

1. We experience certain activating events.

2. We mentally evaluate those events.

3. We experience an emotional response.

If what we believe does not reflect truth (if we draw inaccurate conclusions), then what we feel will not reflect reality.

Consideration

Faith is God's way, and reason is man's way. Faith is not unreasonable, because God is a rational God and does work through our reason. The problem is that man's ability to reason is limited. That is why we are instructed, "Trust in the Lord with all your heart, and do not lean on your own understanding" (Proverbs 3:5). Consciously or subconsciously, we have two plans in our minds.

- Plan A is God's way, which we can choose by faith. Will we choose plan A? That depends on two things: (1) our conviction that God's way is right and (2) our level of commitment to obey God.

- Plan B is reasoning independent of God; it's humanity's tendency to rationalize. Will we choose plan B? That is determined by the amount of time we spend entertaining thoughts that are contrary to the Word of God. Sometimes we consider using plan B as an escape route should plan A fail! When we don't see things God's way, we approach them our way.

Strongholds

Strongholds are habitual ways of thinking that have been burned into our minds, either gradually over time or from the intensity of traumatic experiences. Some call them flesh patterns or defense mechanisms. Strongholds can include inferiority complexes, homosexuality, and problems related to being the adult children of alcoholics.

DISCUSSION QUESTIONS

1. How do we develop our worldview—our perception of reality?

2. What is the fundamental difference between the brain and the mind?

3. What will happen to our lives if we never deal with our flesh patterns or seek to renew our minds?

4. How does the outer, material person correlate with the inner, immaterial person?

5. We have a choice to believe or not believe the truth. How does making that choice affect the way we feel?

6. Knowing we are saved by faith and sanctified by faith (Galatians 3:1-6), how important is it that we know the truth and speak the truth in love if we wish to grow in Christ and relate to one another in love?

7. Think of a mental stronghold or flesh pattern that has dogged your life or family. What false beliefs perpetuate it?

8. How can strongholds be torn down in Christ?

9. What must happen mentally if we want to grow?

10. Why must we also check for "computer viruses"?

4

THE BATTLE FOR OUR MINDS

The Spirit expressly says that in later times some will depart from the faith
by devoting themselves to deceitful spirits and teachings of demons.

1 TIMOTHY 4:1

LESSON OBJECTIVE

To understand the spiritual battle for our minds so we can take every thought captive in obedience to Christ.

Satan, the Deceiver

If the development of strongholds is just a question of conditioning, we could be reconditioned simply through the process of education, counseling, or self-directed study of God's Word. Certainly that is the major process—but is something else going on in the spiritual world as well?

Is Satan capable of putting thoughts in our minds?

- "Then Satan stood up against Israel and moved David to number Israel" (1 Chronicles 21:1 NASB).

- "And supper being ended, the devil having already put it into the heart of Judas Iscariot, Simon's son, to betray him…" (John 13:2 NKJV).

- "But Peter said, 'Ananias, why has Satan filled your heart to lie to the Holy Spirit and to keep back some of the price of the land?'" (Acts 5:3 NASB).

Understanding Our Thoughts (*noema*)

- "Anyone whom you forgive, I also forgive. Indeed, what I have forgiven, if I have forgiven anything, has been for your sake in the presence of Christ, so that we would not be outwitted by Satan; for we are not ignorant of his designs [*noema*]" (2 Corinthians 2:10-11).

- "Even if our gospel is veiled, it is veiled only to those who are perishing. In their case the god of this world has blinded the minds [*noema*] of the unbelievers, to keep them from seeing the light of the gospel of the glory of Christ, who is the image of God" (2 Corinthians 4:3-4).

- "I am afraid that as the serpent deceived Eve by his cunning, your thoughts [*noema*] will be led astray from a sincere and pure devotion to Christ" (2 Corinthians 11:3).

Taking a pill to heal your body is commendable. Taking a pill to heal your soul is deplorable. God help us to know the difference.

Destroying Strongholds

1. Be transformed by renewing your mind (Romans 12:2).

   - Study (2 Timothy 2:15).

   - Let the peace of Christ rule (Colossians 3:15-16).

2. Prepare your minds for action (1 Peter 1:13).

   - Keep your mind active and externally focused.

   - Use your sanctified imagination.

3. Turn to God, who is the truth (Philippians 4:6-7).

4. Choose to think the truth (Philippians 4:8).

5. Live the truth (Philippians 4:9).

We are not called to dispel the darkness. We are called to turn on the light.

DISCUSSION QUESTIONS

1. Why is deception the major strategy of Satan, the father of lies?

2. If Satan is capable of putting thoughts in our minds, how can we recognize a thought is from him?

3. Why do we need to take every thought captive to the obedience of Christ?

4. Can blasphemous and condemning thoughts be treated by medication? Why or why not?

5. How can we tell the difference between mental illness and a spiritual battle for the mind?

6. The Greek word translated *anxiety* in the New Testament comes from two root words that mean "divide" and "mind." How can we overcome double mindedness according to Philippians 4:6-7? (See also Matthew 6:24-25,33; James 1:6-8; 1 Peter 5:7.)

7. Can we simply choose to not think negative thoughts? Why or why not?

8. What should we do with our minds?

5

Managing Our Emotional Life

*"Let each one of you speak truth with his neighbor," for we are
members of one another. "Be angry, and do not sin": do not let the
sun go down on your wrath, nor give place to the devil.*

Ephesians 4:25-27 nkjv

*[Cast] all your anxiety on Him, because He cares for you.
Be of sober spirit, be on the alert. Your adversary, the devil, prowls
around like a roaring lion, seeking someone to devour.*

1 Peter 5:7-8 nasb

LESSON OBJECTIVE

To understand our emotional nature in order to live as real people and
bring healing to damaged emotions.

How Do We Respond to Our Emotions?

Our emotional state also affects the way we live. Emotions have been likened to a red warning light on the instrument panel of a car. We can put a piece of tape over the light (suppression), smash it with a hammer (indiscriminate expression), or look under the hood (acknowledgment).

Suppression

- Suppressing our emotions is unhealthy and can be the root of psychosomatic illnesses (Psalm 32; 39:1-3).

- Suppressing our emotions is also dishonest (Proverbs 10:18; 13:10). If people have to guess what we're feeling, they will usually guess wrong, and presumption leads to strife.

Indiscriminate Expression

Suppressing our emotions is unhealthy for us, and expressing them indiscriminately (blowing up) is unhealthy for others (James 1:19).

Acknowledgment

- Emotional honesty begins with being honest with God (Psalm 109:1-15). We must be real in order to be right with God.

- Emotional honesty is necessary for effective ministry to others (Job 6:24-26; Romans 12:15). Learn to respond not to people's words, but to what they are actually feeling.

- Emotional honesty is also necessary for effective relationships (Ephesians 4:25-27). We can honestly tell others about our feelings instead of blowing up at them. This lets them off the hook. Instead of responding defensively to our outbursts, they can lovingly meet our emotional needs.

Knowing Our Emotional Limits

We manage our emotions by managing our thought life. When we take note of our thoughts, address the lies, and replace them with more accurate, helpful ways of thinking, our emotions will settle down. "My endurance has perished; so has my hope from the LORD…But this I call to *mind*, and therefore I have hope: The steadfast love of the LORD never ceases; his mercies never come to an end; they are new every morning; great is your faithfulness" (Lamentations 3:18,21-23).

This is not usually too difficult to do with present circumstances, but what if we have emotional baggage from our past?

Scripture uses the word *heart* 822 times to refer to the human personality. Of those usages, 204 refer to intellectual activity, 195 to the will, and 166 to emotions. The heart is the real person (Proverbs 27:19) and the place from which all life flows (Proverbs 4:23). The heart is the place of personhood, intellect, emotion, and will. God promised in Ezekiel 36:26 (NIV), "I will give you a new heart and put a new spirit in you."

How the Past Affects Us Emotionally

Long-standing emotional traumas from the past can be triggered by present events or by our reminiscing. This is the way the sequence normally works:

1. Past experiences establish primary emotions.

2. A present event triggers a primary emotion.

3. We mentally evaluate present circumstances (management stage).

4. A secondary emotion is a combination of our thoughts and primary emotions.

Some people avoid other people, places, and events that may trigger primary emotions, but what they need is to be free from their past. Here's how that can happen:

1. *Become a new creation in Christ.* You are not primarily a product of your past; you are a new creation in Christ, a product of Christ's work on the cross and His resurrection. Nobody can fix your past, but you can be free from it by the grace of God.

2. *Allow the truth to enter your heart* (Psalm 51:6). Thinking, feeling, and willing all come together in the heart in holistic unity. Our emotions are determined by the way our minds were programmed by past events. As new creations in Christ with new hearts and the mind of Christ, we reprocess the past events that left us with emotional bondage. Those past traumas do not keep us in bondage. The lies we have believed as a result of the traumas are what keep us in bondage.

3. *Choose to forgive from your heart* (Matthew 18:35).

DISCUSSION QUESTIONS

1. What may happen if we suppress our emotions?

2. What are some potential consequences of indiscriminately displaying our emotions?

3. How should we acknowledge our emotions to God? With others?

4. How can emotional dishonesty affect relationships?

5. What should we do when we reach our emotional limits?

6. Share an example of how a primary emotion from your past was triggered by some present event.

7. How does emotional baggage from our past mingle with present day reality?

8. How can we become emotionally free from our past?

6

THE FREEDOM OF FORGIVENESS

Forgive us our debts, as we also have forgiven our debtors.

MATTHEW 6:12

LESSON OBJECTIVE

To understand what it means to forgive from the heart in order that we may do so.

The Need to Forgive

1. God requires that we forgive others because our relationship with Him and our relationship with others are inextricably linked (Matthew 6:9-15).

2. We forgive others for our own good. Forgiving others is essential if we are to be free (Matthew 18:21-35).

- Remembering the extent of our own debt will motivate us to forgive others (Luke 7:47).

- We could never repay our debt to God, yet He forgave us. Likewise, we can forgive others even if we feel they could never repay their "debt" to us.

- We can extend mercy to others as God has extended mercy to us. Mercy is "not getting what we deserve." Similarly, we can give grace to others as God has given us grace. Grace is "getting what we don't deserve."

- When we forgive, we do not allow Satan to take advantage of us (2 Corinthians 2:10-11).

3. Though we must extend forgiveness to others (Ephesians 4:31-32), the crisis of forgiveness is between us and God.

4. Why should we forgive? *To stop the pain!* We don't heal in order to forgive; we forgive in order to heal.

What Is Forgiveness?

- Forgiving is not forgetting. When the Bible says God does not remember our sins, it means He does not use the past against us. Forgetting is not a means to forgiveness, but it may be a long-term by-product.

- Forgiving is not tolerating sin. We must set scriptural boundaries in order to stop further abuse. However, we do not retaliate in kind.

- When we forgive, we do not seek resentment, revenge, or repayment. We can leave revenge to God and be assured that someday, all things will be made right. Harboring bitterness is like taking poison and hoping the other person will die. To forgive is to set a captive free and then realize that you were the captive.

- When we forgive, we resolve to live with the consequences of others' sin.

- When we forgive, we may wonder, where is the justice? Justice was served at the cross!

Steps to Forgiveness

- Make a list of the people who have offended you. List as many as you can remember.

- Face the hurt and the hate. Don't suppress your feelings. Instead, honestly identify them.

- Decide that you will bear the burden of others' sin against you and not hold it against them.

- Take others' sin and your pain to the cross.

- Choose to let them go.

DISCUSSION QUESTIONS

1. Can we have a right relationship with God in exclusion of others? Why or why not?

2. If you have offended someone else, where should you go and what should you do? (See Matthew 5:23-25.)

3. If you have been offended by someone else, whom should you go to?

4. Why is it unadvisable and sometimes impossible to go to the offender?

5. What is the difference between justice, mercy, and grace?

6. What is the difference between forgetting and forgiving?

7. Are you tolerating sin when you forgive others?

8. Why is it right to set up scriptural boundaries to stop further abuse?

9. Why should you let offenders off your hook?

10. What did Christ do when He forgave you, and how can we do likewise?

Part 2

THE BELIEVER'S POSITION, AUTHORITY, AND PROTECTION IN CHRIST

THE POSITION OF THE BELIEVER

We were buried therefore with him by baptism into death,
in order that, just as Christ was raised from the dead by the
glory of the Father, we too might walk in newness of life.

ROMANS 6:4

LESSON OBJECTIVE

To understand the practical significance of our position in Christ so we
can live victoriously over sin and death.

Your Identification with Christ (Romans 6:1-10)

When you find a promise, claim it. When you find a command, obey it. When you find a
fact, believe it.

In these ten verses, the verbs describing our position in Christ are past tense. They describe
events that have already happened. We cannot do for ourselves what Christ has already done for
us. We cannot die to sin (6:2) because born-again believers already have died to sin.

We are identified with all parts of Christ's life:

- His death (Romans 6:3,6; Galatians 2:20; Colossians 3:1-3)
- His burial (Romans 6:4)
- His resurrection (Romans 6:5,8,11)
- His ascension (Ephesians 2:6)
- His life (Romans 5:10-11)
- His power (Romans 8:16-17; Ephesians 1:11-12)

Our identity in Christ is a question of knowledge, not experience (Romans 6:6,9). Many Christians feel powerless over sin, so they falsely reason, "What experience must I have in order for this to be true?" They try to become somebody they already are! Others try to put the old self to death, but they can't because he is already dead! We walk by faith according to what God says is true, and then that truth works out in our experience. Trying to make something true by our experience will only lead to frustration.

The goal of our identification with Christ is to walk in newness of life, having power over death and over sin.

You Are Dead to Sin (Romans 6:11)

You do not make yourself dead to sin by considering yourself so. You consider it so because God says it is already so.

- Death is the ending of a relationship, not annihilation.

- The power of sin has not died. (See Romans 8:1-2.)

Romans 6:1-11 teaches that what is true about the Lord Jesus is true of our relationship to sin and death because of our union with Him. God the Father turned His back on His only Son and "made Him who knew no sin to be sin on our behalf, so that we might become the righteousness of God in Him" (2 Corinthians 5:21 NASB). Jesus died to sin once and for all. We are to consider it so for ourselves because of our union with Him—because it *is* so. We have died once and for all time to the realm, rule, and reign of sin and death. Death has no dominion over us. We have been transported out of the domain of darkness and transferred to the kingdom of His beloved Son (Colossians 1:13). This is not made true by experience, nor is it a command to be obeyed. Rather, it is a blessed spiritual fact to be believed. We believe the truth in order for it to work out in our experience. God saves us in order to bring us back to the state in which He originally created Adam and to present us pure, spotless, and undefiled (Ephesians 5:27). Sin is neither dead nor powerless; we are still capable of sinning. But we are not slaves to sin, and we are not under the dominion of sin.

Your Mortal Body and Your Self (Romans 6:12)

You can allow sin to reign in your mortal body, but you don't have to. In fact, not letting sin reign in your mortal body is your responsibility.

- You are more than your physical body (Philippians 3:20-21).

- Whatever is mortal is corruptible (1 Corinthians 15:42-45).

Exercise Your Will (Romans 6:13-14)

Paul gives one negative command: Do not present your body to sin as an instrument of unrighteousness. He also gives two positive commands: Present yourself to God, and present your body to God as an instrument of righteousness.

You are under the grace of God and not the law (6:11-12).

What If Sin Reigned? (Romans 7:15-25)

This passage demonstrates that applying the law will not get people out of bondage. Every disposition of the person's heart in this passage is toward God. He knows what is right and wants to do what is right. Neither of these are true of unbelievers. Some no-good thing is dwelling in him, but it is not him. Evil is lying close at hand, but he is not evil. The sin that dwells within him (verse 20) is waging war against his mind, which is where the battle is. No one is more miserable than the person who knows what is right and wants to do what is right but can't seem to do it. Who will set this person free?

To illustrate the tension in Romans 7:15-25, consider those who are struggling with eating disorders. Why do they starve themselves, binge and purge, and defecate? They do these things because they believe evil is present in them—but such means will not cleanse them. They have to renounce such behaviors and trust only in the cleansing work of Christ.

Christians who have committed sexual sins have allowed sin to reign in their mortal bodies. They need to renounce sexual acts with others and ask God to break the bonds because they have joined themselves to others and have become one flesh with them (1 Corinthians 6:15-18). You will be given an opportunity to do this in the Steps to Freedom at the end of the video series. For more information about overcoming sexual strongholds and sexual abuse, read my book *Winning the Battle Within* (Harvest House, 2008).

DISCUSSION QUESTIONS

1. Why do we seem to connect with Christ in His death but not in His resurrection?

2. What happens if we believers try to die to sin or put the old self to death?

3. How should we appropriate the finished work of Christ?

4. According to the Galatian heresy (Galatians 3:16), we are saved by faith but perfected by the works of the law. Why is this wrong? How are we perfected?

5. The law of sin and the law of death cannot be done away with, so how do we overcome such laws? (See Romans 8:1-2.)

6. Why is understanding who we are in Christ so important?

7. Why should we consider ourselves to be dead to sin?

8. Whose responsibility is it to not let sin reign in our mortal bodies?

9. What happens if we commit a sexual sin?

10. According to Romans 7:15-25, what would it be like if we allowed sin to reign in our mortal bodies?

THE AUTHORITY OF THE BELIEVER

I pray…that you will know…the surpassing greatness of
His power toward us who believe. These are in accordance
with the working of the strength of His might.

EPHESIANS 1:18-19 NASB

LESSON OBJECTIVE

To understand every believer's authority in Christ and the power that comes from submitting to Him in order to overcome the evil one, who is the god of this world.

The Source of Authority and Power

Because of our position in Christ, we have power and authority (Luke 9:1-2; 10:19-20). Authority is the right to rule; power is the ability to rule. *Subjection* means "to arrange under." Paul prayed that we would be able to see…

- "the surpassing greatness of [God's] *power* [*dunameos*]…
- in accordance with the *working* [*energeian*]
- of the *strength* [*kratous*]
- of His *might* [*ischuous*]" (Ephesians 1:19).

We appropriate Christ's power and authority (Matthew 28:18; Hebrews 8:1). "[God] raised Him from the dead and seated Him at His right hand in the heavenly places, far above all rule and authority and power and dominion, and every name that is named, not only in this age but also in the one to come" (Ephesians 1:20-21). Notice the incredible scope of the Lord's authority!

God Confers Authority on Believers (Ephesians 2:1,5)

Paul admonished us to be strong in the Lord and in the strength of His might (Ephesians 6:10). True believers have both the authority and the power to do His will. Always keep in mind that we are functioning by faith according to His authority and His power in order to do His will.

The Location of Authority (Ephesians 1:20; Hebrews 8:1)

The right hand of the throne of God is the center of authority and the power of the whole universe, and the exercise of the power of the throne was committed to the ascended Lord. The elevation of His people with Him to the heavenlies (spiritual realm) means that they share His authority. They share His throne as joint heirs (Romans 8:17)!

The Rebel Holder of Authority

- Satan is the ruler of this world (Luke 4:6; John 12:31; 14:30; 16:11).
- Satan is the prince of the power of the air (Ephesians 2:2).
- The whole world lies in the power of the evil one (1 John 5:19).
- Satan's rebellious rule includes a hierarchy (Ephesians 6:12).

In Scripture, the terms *rulers* and *authorities* can refer to human individuals in authority, human authority systems (Luke 12:11; Acts 4:26), or superhuman powers (Romans 8:38; Ephesians 6:12; Colossians 1:16; 2:15). The context of Ephesians 6 clearly refers to spiritual entities in "the heavenlies," or the spiritual realm. That does not mean these rulers and powers do not affect human government and agencies; they most certainly do.

Qualifications for Authority

- belief (Ephesians 1:19)
- humility, which is confidence properly placed (James 4:6-7; 1 Peter 5:5-9)
- boldness (Joshua 1:6-7,9,18; Proverbs 28:1; Acts 4:31; Ephesians 3:12-13; Revelation 21:6-8)

Take note that ours is not an independent authority (Acts 19:13-17). Also, this authority is not over each other (Ephesians 5:21). We have the authority to do God's will—nothing more and nothing less.

DISCUSSION QUESTIONS

1. Matthew 28:18-19 reads, "All authority in heaven and on earth has been given to me. Go therefore and make disciples of all nations." How much authority does Satan have on this planet, and what is the significance of that?

2. Why must people have authority before they issue commands?

3. Why is authority (the right to rule) so important in the spiritual realm, and what practical benefit is that for every believer?

4. According to Ephesians 1–2, what has been extended to believers?

5. What is the scope of our power and authority in Christ?

6. Why is it so important for believers to not respond in the flesh and to exercise their God-given authority by taking their position in Christ?

7. Why does Satan want to be feared?

8. What qualifies us to exercise God's authority?

9. Do we have the authority to do our own will?

10. Whom do we have authority over?

THE PROTECTION OF THE BELIEVER

*My prayer is not that you take them out of the world
but that you protect them from the evil one.*

JOHN 17:15

To understand the provision God has made for believers so they will be kept from the evil one and stand firm in their faith.

The Need for Resolution

When people first step into the kingdom of God, how do they respond to voices of temptation and despair?

Some people believe the lies, give up, and go no further into kingdom living. This is why we don't see more evidence of the spiritual battle. Satan is content to be quiet if people's problems are not being resolved. Christianity is not addition (adding Christ to your life); it is transformation, and appropriation requires genuine repentance.

Other people step into the kingdom of God and then begin to interact with the tempting and accusing voices. This seems commendable at first, but in effect, Satan is setting the agenda of their lives, so they don't grow either.

Finally, others put up the shield of faith, ignore the deceiver's lies, and progress on the path to maturity. But people can do this only if they have resolved the issues in their lives.

The Sufficiency of Our Protection in Christ

We have all the protection we need in Christ. "Be strong in the Lord and in the strength of His might" (Ephesians 6:10 NASB).

Romans 13:12-14 identifies the armor with Christ. Satan has nothing in Christ (John 14:30). To the extent that we put on Christ, the evil one cannot touch us (1 John 5:18). He can only touch what is on a level with him; therefore, Paul tells us in Romans 13:14, "Make no provision for the flesh" (his level). The armor does not cover what is contrary to Christ.

The Need for Active Participation

Notice by the verb tenses in Ephesians 6:14-15 that we have already put on the first three pieces of armor. They are ours because we are in Christ. We must continue to believe and to appropriate them. This appropriation requires our active participation (Ephesians 6:11-14 NASB).

- "put on" and "take up" (verses 11,13)

- "stand firm" (verses 11,13-14)

- "be able" (verse 13)

"The chief condition for the working of evil spirits in a human being, apart from sin, is passivity, in exact opposition to the condition which God requires from His children for His working in them."

Jesse Penn-Lewis

The Armor of God (Ephesians 6:14-17)

To put on the armor of God is to put on Christ. Rather than worrying about whether you've put on each piece of armor, simply take your place in Christ. In Him you have...

1. the belt of truth (verse 14)

2. the breastplate of righteousness (verse 14)

3. shoes for the feet in readiness given by the gospel of peace (verse 15)

4. the shield of faith (verse 16)

5. the helmet of salvation (verse 17)

6. the sword of the Spirit, which is the Word of God (verse 17)

DISCUSSION QUESTIONS

1. Why do we need to know about germs and demons?

2. What should our focus be?

3. When you put on the armor of God, what or whom are you actually putting on? Explain.

4. What is our sanctuary?

5. Can we passively take our place in Christ? Why or why not?

6. When we step out of the kingdom of darkness through the Door (Christ) into the kingdom of God's beloved Son, how should we respond to the devil's lies, temptations, and accusations?

7. Why may it be necessary to verbally speak the Word of God?

8. The Lord prays for all of us to be one in Christ. Consider how the devil will seek to divide our minds, our marriages, and the body of Christ.

10

THE VULNERABILITY
OF THE BELIEVER

*There are two equal and opposite errors into which our race can fall about
demons. One is to disbelieve in their existence. The other is to believe and
feel an unhealthy interest in them. They themselves are equally pleased by
both errors and hail a materialist or a magician with the same delight.*

C.S. LEWIS, *THE SCREWTAPE LETTERS*

LESSON OBJECTIVE

To understand the degree of our spiritual vulnerability to the devil's
temptations, accusations, and deceptions so we can know how to stand
against them.

Degrees of Vulnerability

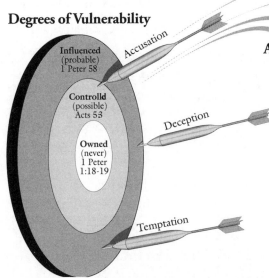

Accusation (Zechariah 3:1-10)

- The Lord rebukes Satan (verse 2). How can
  we tell the difference between Satan's accusations and the Holy Spirit's conviction (see
  2 Corinthians 7:8-10)? Conviction from the
  Holy Spirit leads to repentance, freedom, and
  a life without regret. Condemnation is not
  from God, but from the enemy. For example,
  Judas betrayed Christ, and his sense of condemnation led to suicide. Peter denied Christ
  three times, but his conviction led to repentance and freedom.

49

- The Lord removes Joshua's filthy garments (Zechariah 3:3-5).

- The Lord admonishes Joshua to walk in His ways and perform His service (verses 6-10).

Many Christians wonder whether they have committed the unpardonable sin, or blasphemy of the Holy Spirit (Matthew 12:31-32). But no Christian can commit the unpardonable sin. In Christ, all are forgiven. If unbelievers harden their hearts, committing the sin of unbelief (thus rejecting the unique work of the Holy Spirit to draw all mankind to Christ), they never come to Christ, whose unique work was to die—once for all—for the forgiveness of sins.

TEMPTATION (1 CORINTHIANS 10:13)

Channel of Temptation (1 John 2:15-17)	Lust of the Flesh (animal appetites, cravings, passions) "the woman saw that the tree was good for food" (Genesis 3:6)	Lust of the Eyes (selfishness, self-interest) "and that it was a delight to the eyes" (Genesis 3:6)	Pride of Life (self-promotion, self-exaltation) "and that the tree was desirable to make one wise" (Genesis 3:6)
Draws us away from the	Will of God (Galatians 16:18)	Word of God (Matthew 16:24-26)	Worship of God (1 Peter 5:5-11)
Destroys our	Dependence upon God (John 15:5)	Confidence in God (John 15:7)	Obedience to God (John 15:8-10)
First Adam (Genesis 3:1-6)	"Indeed, has God said, 'You shall not eat from any tree of the garden'?" (Genesis 3:1)	"You surely shall not die!" (Genesis 3:4)	"You will be like God" (Genesis 3:5)
Last Adam (Matthew 4:1-11)	"Man does not live by bread alone, but man lives by everything that proceeds out of the mouth of the LORD" (Deuteronomy 8:3)	"You shall not put the LORD your God to the test" (Deuteronomy 6:16)	"You shall fear only the LORD your God; and you shall worship Him" (Deuteronomy 6:13)

Assurance of Salvation (1 John 5:13)

DECLARATION

Today I call upon the name of the Lord for my salvation. I believe in my heart that God the Father raised Jesus from the dead in order that I might have eternal life. I now declare Him to be the Lord of my life. I renounce any effort on my part to save myself, and I renounce all the accusations of Satan that would rob me of my full assurance of eternal life. I have been transferred out of the kingdom of darkness into the kingdom of His beloved Son. I choose to believe that I am now a child of God who is seated with Him in the heavenlies because of the finished work of Christ.

Signed _____

DISCUSSION QUESTIONS

1. To what degree are Christians vulnerable?

2. What is Satan trying to accomplish by tempting us?

3. Eve was deceived and believed a lie when she hadn't yet sinned. Can people be deceived today? How can we prevent that from happening?

4. Why are we so easily lured away by esoteric knowledge and power?

5. How is Christ protecting us from Satan's accusations?

6. How can we know the difference between Satan's accusations and the conviction of the Holy Spirit?

7. Does God want us to be assured of our salvation? How?

8. Can a Christian commit the unpardonable sin? Why or why not?

SETTING CAPTIVES FREE, PART ONE

Is anyone among you suffering? Then he must pray...
Is anyone among you sick? Then he must call for the elders
of the church... Therefore, confess your sins to one another,
and pray for one another so that you may be healed.

JAMES 5:13-16

LESSON OBJECTIVE

To understand who is responsible for what, so effective ministry can bring about the desired result of setting captives free and binding up the brokenhearted.

Who Is Responsible for What?

Only God can do some things. But God will not do for us what He has told us to do ourselves.

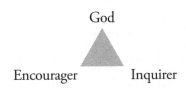

Each side of the triangle represents a relationship. When we help people, our ultimate goal is for them to connect with God.

What Are the Responsibilities of the Inquirers? (James 5:13-16)

1. They must pray (verse 13).

- There is only one mediator between God and humanity (1 Timothy 2:5).

- There are no secondhand relationships between a Father and His children.

- Nobody else can do your praying for you.

- Intercessory prayer is not intended to replace an individual's responsibility to pray.

2. They must take the initiative and assume responsibility for their own well-being (James 5:14). Sick people are to call for the elders.

3. They must be willing to be honest with God (verse 16).

- "Beloved, I pray that in all respects you may prosper and be in good health, *just as your soul prospers*" (3 John 2 NASB).

- "Delight yourself in the LORD, and he will give you the desires of your heart" (Psalm 37:4).

DISCUSSION QUESTIONS

1. Why is it so important to understand who is responsible for what?

2. Have you ever tried to play the role of God in someone's else's life? How did that work?

3. Have you ever tried to usurp another's person's responsibility? How did that work?

4. Why is it so essential that God be included in the discipleship counseling process?

5. Can your problems by resolved by just having another person pray for you? Why or why not?

6. Why must all children of God assume responsibility for their own attitudes and actions?

7. When can we expect our prayers for others to be effective?

8. What is your definition of prosperity? What does prosperity depend on?

9. What will happen if we delight ourselves in the Lord?

10. How will this lesson affect your relationship with God?

12

SETTING CAPTIVES FREE, PART TWO

And the Lord's servant must not be quarrelsome but kind to everyone, able to teach, patiently enduring evil, correcting his opponents with gentleness. God may perhaps grant them repentance leading to a knowledge of the truth, and they may come to their senses and escape from the snare of the devil, after being captured by him to do his will.

2 TIMOTHY 2:24-26

LESSON OBJECTIVE

To understand who is responsible for what so effective ministry can bring about the desired result of setting captives free and binding up the brokenhearted.

The Big Picture

Prior to the cross, Satan was not disarmed, and he ruled as the god of this world. Only a specially endowed authority agent (like Jesus) could expel a demon. Jesus disarmed Satan at the cross, and every believer after Pentecost has the same position and authority in Christ. Believers need to learn how to exercise their authority in Christ and assume responsibility for their own attitudes and actions. Overcoming the enemy is no longer a power encounter. It is a truth encounter. Truth sets people free, and to appropriate that, all believers must repent and believe in God. The encourager helps them do that and thus fulfills the ministry of reconciliation.

The Encourager's Responsibility (2 Timothy 2:24-26)

1. Be the Lord's servant who does not usurp His role and remains totally dependent upon Him.

2. Do not be quarrelsome.

3. Kindness is the essential prerequisite. "What is desirable in a man is his kindness" (Proverbs 19:22 NASB).

4. Be able to teach. That is, bring truth to bear on the situation.

5. Be patient.

   • How many are willing to share all the "dirt" in their lives just for the purpose of sharing it?

   • How many are willing to share all the "dirt" in their lives for the purpose of gaining some understanding as to why they are all "screwed up"?

   • How many are willing to share all the "dirt" in their lives for the purpose of resolving their problems?

6. Be gentle.

7. God is the one who grants repentance.

DISCUSSION QUESTIONS

1. Why would it take an outside agent (such as Christ or the disciples) to free a person from demonic influences under the old covenant?

2. Why is it no longer the outside agent's responsibility to effect someone's freedom under the new covenant?

3. Why is simply resisting the devil not enough?

4. Who can help others find their freedom in Christ? Are certain gifts required? Is this a special office of the church?

5. What does quarreling lead to?

6. Why does one need to be kind?

7. Why are people so reluctant to share their deepest secrets with others?

8. Why do hurting people need kind and gentle helpers?

9. Who is the one who grants repentance?

10. What is the difference between a truth encounter and a power encounter?

Part 3

The Steps
to Freedom in Christ

13

PREPARATION AND STEP 1:
COUNTERFEIT VS. REAL

Resolving Personal and Spiritual Conflicts

We are all born dead (spiritually) in our trespasses and sin (Ephesians 2:1); we have neither the presence of God nor the knowledge of His ways. Consequently, we all learned to live independently of God. When we became new creations in Christ, our minds were not instantly renewed. That is why the apostle Paul wrote, "Do not conform any longer to the pattern of this world, but be transformed by the renewing of your mind. Then you will be able to test and approve what God's will is—his good, pleasing and perfect will" (Romans 12:2 NIV). That is also why new Christians struggle with many of the same old thoughts and habits. Their minds have been previously programmed to live independently of God, and that is the characteristic of our old nature or flesh. As new creations in Christ, we have the mind of Christ, and the Holy Spirit will lead us into all truth.

To experience our freedom in Christ and grow in the grace of God requires repentance, which literally means a change of mind. These Steps to Freedom are designed to help you repent and experience a new way of thinking.

James 4:7 reads, "Submit yourselves therefore to God. Resist the devil, and he will flee from you." Submitting to God is the critical issue. He is the wonderful counselor and the one who grants repentance leading to a knowledge of the truth (2 Timothy 2:24-26).

The Steps to Freedom cover seven critical issues that serve as barriers to our intimacy with God. We will not experience our freedom in Christ if we seek false guidance, believe lies, fail to forgive others as we have been forgiven, live in rebellion, respond in pride, fail to acknowledge our sin, or continue in the sins of our ancestors. "Whoever conceals his transgressions will not prosper, but he who confesses and forsakes [renounces] them will obtain mercy" (Proverbs 28:13). "Therefore, having this ministry by the mercy of God, we do not lose heart. But we have renounced disgraceful, underhanded ways. We refuse to practice cunning or to tamper with God's word, but by the open statement of the truth we would commend ourselves to everyone's conscience in the sight of God" (2 Corinthians 4:1-2).

Even though Satan is disarmed, he still rules this world through a hierarchy of demons who tempt, accuse, and deceive those who fail to put on the armor of God, stand firm in their faith, and take every thought captive to the obedience of Christ. Our sanctuary is our identity and position in Christ, and we have all the protection we need to live a victorious life. But if we fail to assume our responsibility and we give ground to Satan, we will suffer the consequences of our sinful attitudes and actions. The good news is, we can repent and reclaim all that we have in Christ, and that is what these Steps to Freedom will enable you to do.

Processing the Steps

The best way to go through the Steps is to process them with a trained encourager. The book *Discipleship Counseling* (Regal Books, 2003) explains the theology and process. You can also go through the Steps on your own. Every step is explained so you will have no trouble doing that. I suggest you find a quiet place where you can process the Steps out loud.

If you experience some mental interference, such as, "This isn't going to work," "I don't believe this," or other blasphemous, condemning, or accusing thoughts, just ignore those thoughts and continue on. They have no power over you unless you believe them. They are just thoughts, and whether they originate from yourself, from an external source, or from evil spirits is not important. The issue will be resolved when you have fully repented. If you are working with a trained encourager, share any mental or physical opposition that you are experiencing. The mind is the control center, and you will not lose control in the counseling session if you don't lose control of your mind. The best way to do that, if you are being mentally harassed, is to simply share it. Exposing the lies to the light breaks their power.

If you are processing these Steps in a group, the leader will guide you through the process. You will pray together out loud as a group and then be given some time to process each step yourself. These are issues between yourself and God. You can always submit to God inwardly because He knows the thoughts and intentions of your heart. Resisting the devil will be done verbally as a group when finishing the Steps. Nobody will be embarrassed and asked to reveal any details of their lives. Just don't pay attention to any interference from the enemy.

Remember, you are a child of God and are seated with Christ in the heavenlies. That means you have the authority and power to do His will. The Steps don't set you free—Jesus sets you free, and you will progressively experience that freedom as you respond to Him in faith and repentance. Don't worry about any demonic interference—most people do not experience any. Regardless of whether Satan has a little role or a bigger role, the critical issue is your relationship with God, and that is what you are resolving. This is a ministry of reconciliation. Once those issues are resolved, Satan has no right to remain.

Successfully completing this repentance process is not an end; it is a beginning of growth. Unless these issues are resolved, however, the growth process will be stalled, and your Christian life will be stagnant.

Preparation

Processing these Steps will play a major role in your continuing process of sanctification, which is God's will for your life (1 Thessalonians 4:3). The purpose is to get you firmly rooted in Christ. It doesn't take long to establish your identity and freedom in Christ, but there is no such thing as instant maturity. Renewing your mind and conforming to the image of God is a life-long process. May the Lord grace you with His presence as you seek to do His will. Once you have experienced your freedom in Christ, you can help others experience the joy of their salvation. Begin the Steps with the following prayer and declaration.

PRAYER

> Dear heavenly Father, You are present in this room and in my life. You alone are all-knowing, all-powerful, and everywhere present, and I worship You alone. I declare my dependency upon You, for apart from You I can do nothing. I choose to believe Your Word, which teaches that all authority in heaven and earth belongs to the resurrected Christ, and being alive in Christ, I have the authority to resist the devil as I submit to You. I ask that You fill me with Your Holy Spirit and guide me into all truth. I ask for Your complete protection and guidance as I seek to know You and do Your will. In the wonderful name of Jesus I pray. Amen.

DECLARATION

> In the name and authority of the Lord Jesus Christ, I command Satan and all evil spirits to release their hold on me in order that I can be free to know and choose to do the will of God. As a child of God who is seated with Christ in the heavenly places, I declare that every enemy of the Lord Jesus Christ in my presence be bound. Satan and all his demons cannot inflict any pain or in any way prevent God's will from being done in my life today because I belong to the Lord Jesus Christ.

Step One: Counterfeit vs. Real

The first step toward experiencing your freedom in Christ is to renounce (verbally reject) all involvement (past or present) with occult, cult, or false religious teachings or practices. Participation in any group that denies that Jesus Christ is Lord and/or elevates any teaching or book to the level of (or above) the Bible must be renounced. In addition, groups that require dark, secret initiations, ceremonies, vows, pacts, or covenants need to be renounced. God does not take false guidance lightly. "As for the person who turns to mediums and to spiritists…I will also set My face against that person and will cut him off from among his people" (Leviticus 20:6 NASB). You don't want the Lord to cut you off, so ask Him to guide you.

PRAYER

> Dear heavenly Father, please bring to my mind anything and everything that I have done knowingly or unknowingly that involves occult, cult, or false religious teachings or practices. I want to experience Your freedom by renouncing any and all false guidance. In Jesus' name I pray. Amen.

The Lord may bring to your mind experiences that you have forgotten. Even if your participation was thought to be just a game, it is serious and needs to be renounced. You should renounce it even if you passively or curiously watched others participate in counterfeit religious practices. The purpose is to renounce all counterfeit spiritual experiences and their beliefs.

To help bring these things to your mind, prayerfully consider the Non-Christian Spiritual Checklist below. Then pray the prayer following the checklist to renounce each activity or group the Lord brings to mind. He may reveal to you ones that are not on the list. Be especially aware of your need to renounce non-Christian folk religious practices if you have grown up in another culture.

NON-CHRISTIAN SPIRITUAL CHECKLIST
(Check every item you have participated in)

- ☐ out-of-body experiences
- ☐ Bloody Mary
- ☐ spells and curses
- ☐ automatic writing
- ☐ spirit guides
- ☐ tarot cards
- ☐ witchcraft/wicca/sorcery
- ☐ Ouija board
- ☐ Magic Eight Ball
- ☐ mental telepathy/mind control
- ☐ trances
- ☐ fortune telling/divination
- ☐ levitation
- ☐ Satanism

- ☐ palm reading
- ☐ hypnosis
- ☐ seances/mediums/channelers
- ☐ blood pacts
- ☐ sexual spirits
- ☐ superstitions
- ☐ Jehovah Witnesses
- ☐ Christian Science/mind science
- ☐ Unification church (Moonies)
- ☐ Scientology
- ☐ Silva mind control
- ☐ Yoga (the religion, not the exercise)
- ☐ Bahaism
- ☐ Islam
- ☐ Buddhism (including Zen)
- ☐ imaginary friends
- ☐ false gods (money, sex, power, pleasure, people…)
- ☐ astrology/horoscopes
- ☐ astral projection
- ☐ black or white magic
- ☐ fatishism/crystals/charms
- ☐ martial arts (bowing to a divine master)
- ☐ Mormonism, including temple rituals
- ☐ New Age practices and beliefs
- ☐ Masons, including initiation vows
- ☐ The Forum (est)
- ☐ Unitarianism/universalism
- ☐ Transcendental Meditation
- ☐ Hare Krishna
- ☐ Native American spirit worship
- ☐ Hinduism
- ☐ Rosicrucianism
- ☐ vows and pacts (secret or otherwise)
- ☐ other non-Christian religions, cults, or the occult, including their movies, music, and games

Once you have completed your checklist, confess and renounce every false religious practice, belief, ceremony, vow, or pact you were involved in by praying the following prayer aloud.

PRAYER

> Lord Jesus, I confess that I have participated in [specifically name every belief and involvement with all the items you checked above], and I renounce them all as counterfeits. I pray that You will fill me with Your Holy Spirit that I may be guided by You. Thank You that in Christ I am forgiven. Amen.

Satanic Worship

People who have been subjected to satanic ritual abuse (SRA) need the help of someone who understands dissociative disorders and spiritual warfare. If you have been involved in any form of satanic worship, say these Special Renunciations aloud. Read across the page, renouncing the first item in the column under Kingdom of Darkness and then announcing the truth in the column under Kingdom of Light. Continue down the page in that manner. Notice that satanic worship is the antithesis of true worship.

SPECIAL RENUNCIATIONS

KINGDOM OF DARKNESS	KINGDOM OF LIGHT
I renounce ever signing my name over to Satan or having my name signed over to Satan.	I announce that my name is written in the Lamb's book of life.
I renounce any ceremony in which I have been wed to Christ.	I announce that I am the bride of Christ.
I renounce any and all covenants I made with Satan.	I announce that I am under the new covenant of grace.
I renounce any and all satanic assignments for my life, including duties and family.	I announce and commit myself to know and do only the will of God as He guides me.
I renounce all spirit guides assigned to me.	I accept only the leading of the Holy Spirit.
I renounce ever giving my blood in the service of Satan.	I trust only in the shed blood of the Lord Jesus Christ.
I renounce ever eating flesh or drinking blood for satanic worship.	By faith I partake in communion through the body and blood of the Lord Jesus Christ.
I renounce any and all guardians and Satanist parents who were assigned to me.	I announce that God is my Father and the Holy Spirit is my guardian.
I renounce any baptism whereby I have identified with Satan.	I announce that I have been baptized into the Lord Jesus Christ.
I renounce any and all sacrifices that were made on my behalf by which Satan may claim ownership of me.	I announce that only the sacrifice of Christ has any hold on me. I belong to Him. I have been purchased by the blood of the Lamb.

14

STEP 2:
DECEPTION VS. TRUTH

The Christian life is lived by faith according to what God says is true. Jesus is the truth, the Holy Spirit is the Spirit of truth, God's Word is truth, and we are to speak the truth in love (see John 14:6; 16:13; 17:17; Ephesians 4:15). The biblical response to truth is *faith* regardless of whether we *feel* it is true. In addition, Christians are to have no part in lying, deceiving, stretching the truth, or anything else associated with falsehood. Lies keep us in bondage, but truth sets us free (John 8:32). David wrote, "How blessed [happy] is the man...in whose spirit there is no deceit" (Psalm 32:2). Joy and freedom come from walking in the truth.

We find the courage to be transparent before God and others (see 1 John 1:7) when we know that God loves and accepts us just as we are. We can face reality, acknowledge our sins, and not try to hide or cover up. Begin this commitment to walk in the light by praying the following prayer out loud. Don't let any opposing thoughts, such as "This is a waste of time" or "I wish I could believe this, but I can't" keep you from pressing forward. God will strengthen you as you rely on Him.

PRAYER

> Dear heavenly Father, You are the truth, and I desire to live by faith according to Your truth. The truth will set me free, but in many ways I have been deceived by the father of lies and the philosophies of this fallen world, and I have deceived myself. I choose to walk in the light, knowing that You love and accept me just as I am. As I consider areas of possible deception, I invite the Spirit of truth to guide me into all truth. Please protect me from all deception as You "search me, O God, and know my heart; try me and know my anxious thoughts; and see if there be any hurtful way in me, and lead me in the everlasting way" [Psalm 139:23-24 NASB]. In the name of Jesus I pray. Amen.

Prayerfully consider the lists in the three exercises below, using the prayers at the end of each exercise to confess any ways you have given in to deception or wrongly defended yourself. You cannot instantly renew your mind, but the process will never get started without acknowledging our mental strongholds (also called defense mechanisms or flesh patterns).

Deception by the World

- ☐ believing that acquiring money and things will bring lasting happiness (Matthew 13:22; 1 Timothy 6:10)

- ☐ believing that excessive food and alcohol can relieve my stress and make me happy (Proverbs 23:19-21)

- ☐ believing that an attractive body and personality will get me what I need (Proverbs 31:10; 1 Peter 3:3-4)

- ☐ believing that gratifying sexual lust will bring lasting satisfaction (Ephesians 4:22; 1 Peter 2:11)

- ☐ believing that I can sin and not experience any negative consequences (Hebrews 3:12-13)

- ☐ believing that I need more than what God has given me in Christ (2 Corinthians 11:2-4,13-15)

- ☐ believing that I can do whatever I want and no one can touch me (Proverbs 16:18; Obadiah 3;1 Peter 5:5)

- ☐ believing that unrighteous people who refuse to accept Christ go to heaven anyway (1 Corinthians 6:9-11)

- ☐ believing that I can associate with bad company and not become corrupted (1 Corinthians 15:33-34)

- ☐ believing that I can read, see, or listen to anything and not be corrupted (Proverbs 4:23-27; Matthew 5:28)

- ☐ believing that there are no consequences on earth for my sin (Galatians 6:7-8)

- ☐ believing that I must gain the approval of certain people in order to be happy (Galatians 1:10)

- ☐ believing that I must measure up to certain standards in order to feel good about myself (Galatians 3:2-3; 5:1)

PRAYER

> Lord Jesus, I confess that I have been deceived by [confess the items you checked above]. I thank You for Your forgiveness, and I commit myself to believe only Your truth. In Jesus' name I pray. Amen.

Deception by Myself

- ☐ hearing God's Word but not doing what it says (James 1:22)
- ☐ saying I have no sin (1 John 1:8)
- ☐ thinking I am something I'm really not (Galatians 6:3)
- ☐ thinking I am wise in this worldly age (1 Corinthians 3:18-19)
- ☐ thinking I can be truly religious but not bridle my tongue (James 1:26)
- ☐ thinking God is the source of my problems (Lamentations 3)
- ☐ thinking I can live my life without the help of anyone else (1 Corinthians 12:14-20)

PRAYER

> Lord Jesus, I confess that I have deceived myself by [confess the items checked above]. Thank You for Your forgiveness. I commit myself to believe only Your truth. In Jesus' name I pray. Amen.

Defending Myself

- ☐ denial of reality (conscious or unconscious)
- ☐ fantasy (escaping reality through daydreaming, TV, movies, music, computer or video games, drugs, alcohol…)
- ☐ emotional insulation (withdrawing from people or keeping people at a distance to avoid rejection)
- ☐ regression (reverting back to less threatening times)
- ☐ displaced anger (taking out frustrations on innocent people)
- ☐ projection (attributing to another what I find unacceptable in myself)
- ☐ rationalization (making excuses for my own poor behavior)
- ☐ lying (protecting myself through falsehoods)

☐ blaming myself (when not responsible) and others

☐ hypocrisy (presenting a false image)

PRAYER

> Lord Jesus, I confess that I have wrongly defended myself by [confess the items checked above]. Thank You for Your forgiveness. I trust You to defend and protect me. In Jesus' name I pray. Amen.

The wrong ways we have employed to shield ourselves from pain and rejection are often deeply engrained in our lives. You may need additional discipleship counseling to learn how to allow Christ to be your rock, fortress, deliverer, and refuge (see Psalm 18:1-2). The more you learn how loving, powerful, and protective God is, the more you'll be likely to trust Him. The more you realize His complete acceptance of you in Christ, the more you'll be released to be open, honest, and (in a healthy way) vulnerable before God and others.

The New Age movement has twisted the concept of faith by teaching that we make something true by believing it. That is false. We cannot create reality with our minds; only God can do that. Our responsibility is to *face* reality and choose to believe what God says is true. True biblical faith, therefore, is choosing to believe and act upon what is true because God has said it is true and because He is the truth. Faith is something you decide to do, not something you feel like doing. Believing something doesn't make it true; it's already true, therefore we choose to believe it! Truth is not conditioned by whether we choose to believe it.

Everybody lives by faith. The only difference between Christian faith and non-Christian faith is the object of our faith. If the object of our faith is not trustworthy, no amount of believing will change that. That's why our faith must be grounded on the solid rock of God's perfect, unchanging character and the truth of His Word. For two thousand years Christians have known the importance of verbally and publicly declaring truth. Read aloud the following Statements of Truth and carefully consider what you are professing. Reading these aloud daily for several weeks will help renew your mind to the truth.

STATEMENTS OF TRUTH

1. I recognize that there is only one true and living God who exists as the Father, Son, and Holy Spirit. He is worthy of all honor, praise, and glory as the one who made all things and holds all things together. [See Exodus 20:2-3; Colossians 1:16-17.]

2. I recognize that Jesus Christ is the Messiah, the Word who became flesh and dwelt among us. I believe that He came to destroy the works of the devil and that He disarmed the rulers and authorities and made a public display of them, having triumphed over them. [See John 1:1,14; Colossians 2:15; 1 John 3:8.]

3. I believe that God demonstrated His own love for me in that while I was still a sinner, Christ died for me. I believe that He has delivered me from the domain of darkness and transferred me to His kingdom, and in Him I have redemption, the forgiveness of sins. [See Romans 5:8; Colossians 1:13-14.]

4. I believe I am now a child of God and that I am seated with Christ in the heavenlies. I believe that I was saved by the grace of God through faith, and that it was a gift and not a result of any works on my part. [See Ephesians 2:6,8-9; 1 John 3:13.]

5. I choose to be strong in the Lord and in the strength of His might. I put no confidence in the flesh, for the weapons of warfare are not of the flesh but are divinely powerful for the destruction of strongholds. I put on the full armor of God. I resolve to stand firm in my faith and resist the evil one. [See 2 Corinthians 10:4; Ephesians 6:10-20; Philippians 3:3.]

6. I believe that apart from Christ I can do nothing, so I declare my complete dependence on Him. I choose to abide in Christ in order to bear much fruit and glorify my Father. I announce to Satan that Jesus is my Lord. I reject any and all counterfeit gifts or works of Satan in my life. [See John 15:5,8; 1 Corinthians 12:3.]

7. I believe that the truth will set me free and that Jesus is the truth. If He sets me free, I will be free indeed. I recognize that walking in the light is the only path of true fellowship with God and man. Therefore, I stand against all of Satan's deception by taking every thought captive in obedience to Christ. I declare that the Bible is the only authoritative standard for truth and life. [See John 8:32,36; 14:6; 2 Corinthians 10:5; 2 Timothy 3:15-17; 1 John 1:3-7.]

8. I choose to present my body to God as a living and holy sacrifice and the members of my body as instruments of righteousness. I choose to renew my mind by the living Word of God in order that I may prove that the will of God is good, acceptable, and perfect. I put off the old self with its evil practices and put on the new self. I declare myself to be a new creation in Christ. (See Romans 6:13; 12:1-2; 2 Corinthians 5:17; Colossians 3:9-10 NIV.)

9. By faith, I choose to be filled with the Spirit so that I can be guided into all truth. I

choose to walk by the Spirit so that I will not carry out the desires of the flesh. (See John 16:13; Galatians 5:16; Ephesians 5:18.)

10. I renounce all selfish goals and choose the ultimate goal of love. I choose to obey the two greatest commandments: to love the Lord my God with all my heart, soul, mind, and strength, and to love my neighbor as myself. (See Matthew 22:37-39; 1 Timothy 1:5.)

11. I believe that the Lord Jesus has all authority in heaven and on earth, and He is the head over all rule and authority. I am complete in Him. I believe that Satan and his demons are subject to me in Christ since I am a member of Christ's body. Therefore, I obey the command to submit to God and resist the devil, and I command Satan in the name of Jesus Christ to leave my presence. (See Matthew 28:18; Ephesians 1:19-23; Colossians 2:10; James 4:7.)

15

Step 3:
Bitterness vs. Forgiveness

We are called to be merciful, just as our heavenly Father is merciful (Luke 6:36), and to forgive others as we have been forgiven (Ephesians 4:31-32). Doing so sets us free from our past and doesn't allow Satan to take advantage of us (2 Corinthians 2:10-11). Ask God to bring to your mind the people you need to forgive by praying the following prayer aloud.

Prayer

> Dear heavenly Father, I thank You for the riches of Your kindness, forbearance, and patience toward me, knowing that Your kindness has led me to repentance. I confess that I have not shown that same kindness and patience toward those who have hurt or offended me [Romans 2:4]. Instead, I have held on to my anger, bitterness, and resentment toward them. Please bring to my mind all the people I need to forgive in order that I may now do so. In Jesus' name I pray. Amen.

Make a List

On a separate sheet of paper, list the names of people who come to your mind. At this point, don't question whether you need to forgive them. Often we hold things against ourselves as well, punishing ourselves for wrong choices we've made in the past. Write "myself" at the bottom of your list if you need to forgive yourself. Forgiving yourself is accepting the truth that God has already forgiven you in Christ. If God forgives you, you can forgive yourself!

Also write down "thoughts against God" at the bottom of your list. Obviously, God has never done anything wrong, so He doesn't need our forgiveness, but we need to let go of our disappointments with our heavenly Father. People often harbor angry thoughts against Him because

He did not do what they wanted Him to do. Those feelings of anger or resentment toward God need to be released.

Review What Forgiveness Is

Before you begin working through the process of forgiving those on your list, review what forgiveness is and what it is not.

Forgiveness is not forgetting. People who want to forget all that was done to them will find they cannot do it. When God says He will remember our sins no more, He is saying He will not use the past against us. Forgetting is a long-term by-product of forgiveness, but it is never a means toward it. Don't put off forgiving those who have hurt you, hoping the pain will go away. *After* you choose to forgive someone, Christ will heal your wounds. We don't heal in order to forgive; we forgive in order to heal.

Forgiveness is a choice, a decision of the will. God requires you to forgive, so we know that it is something you can do. Some people hold on to their anger as a means of protecting themselves against further abuse, but all they are doing is hurting themselves. Others want revenge. The Bible teaches, "'Vengeance is mine, I will repay,' says the Lord" (Romans 12:19 NASB). Let God deal with the person. Let him or her off your hook because as long as you refuse to forgive someone, you are still hooked to that person. You are still chained to your past, bound up in your bitterness. By forgiving, you let the other person off your hook, but he or she is not off God's hook. You must trust that God will deal with the person justly and fairly, something you simply cannot do.

But you don't know how much this person hurt me! No other human really knows another person's pain, but Jesus does, and He instructs us to forgive others for our sakes. Until you let go of your bitterness and hate, the person is still hurting you. Nobody can fix your past, but you can be free from it. What you gain by forgiving is freedom from your past and from those who have abused you. To forgive is to set a captive free and then realize you were the captive.

Forgiveness is agreeing to live with the consequences of another person's sin. We are all living with the consequences of others' sin. The only choice is to do so either in the bondage of bitterness or in the freedom of forgiveness. But where is the justice? The cross makes forgiveness legally and morally right. Jesus died once for all our sins. We are to forgive as Christ has forgiven us. He did that by taking upon Himself the consequences of our sins. God "made Him who knew no sin to be sin on our behalf, so that we might become the righteousness of God in Him" (2 Corinthians 5:21 NASB). Do not wait for the other person to ask for your forgiveness. Remember, Jesus did not wait for those who were crucifying Him to apologize before He forgave them. Even while they mocked and jeered at Him, He prayed, "Father, forgive them; for they do not know what they are doing" (Luke 23:34 NASB).

Forgive from your heart. Allow God to bring to the surface the painful memories, and acknowledge how you feel toward those who have hurt you. If your forgiveness doesn't touch the emotional core of your life, it will be incomplete. Too often we're afraid of the pain, so we bury our emotions deep down inside us. Let God bring them to the surface so He can begin to heal those damaged emotions.

Forgiveness is choosing not to hold others' sin against them anymore. Bitter people commonly bring up past offenses with those who have hurt them. They want the offenders to feel as bad as they do! But we must let go of the past and choose to reject any thought of revenge. This doesn't mean you continue to put up with the abuse. God does not tolerate sin, and neither should you. You will need to set up scriptural boundaries that put a stop to further abuse. Take a stand against sin while continuing to exercise grace and forgiveness toward those who hurt you. If you need help setting scriptural boundaries to protect yourself from further abuse, talk to a trusted friend, counselor, or pastor.

Don't wait until you feel like forgiving. You will never get there. Make the hard choice to forgive even if you don't feel like it. Once you choose to forgive, Satan will lose his hold on you, and God will heal your damaged emotions.

Make the Choice

Start with the first person on your list and make the choice to forgive him or her for every painful memory that comes to your mind. Stay with that individual until you are sure you have dealt with all the remembered pain. Then work your way down the list in the same way.

As you begin forgiving people, God may bring to your mind painful memories you've totally forgotten. Let Him do this even if it hurts. God is surfacing those painful memories so you can face them once for all time and let them go. Don't excuse others' behavior even if they are close to you.

Don't say, "Lord, please help me to forgive." He is already helping you and will be with you all the way through the process. Don't say, "Lord, I want to forgive," because that bypasses the hard choice we have to make. Say, "Lord, I choose to forgive these people and what they did to me."

For every painful memory that God reveals for each person on your list, pray this prayer aloud.

PRAYER

> Lord Jesus, I choose to forgive [name the person] for [what he or she did or failed to do] because it made me feel [share the painful feelings, such as rejected, dirty, worthless, or inferior].

After you have forgiven every person for every painful memory, pray this prayer as well.

PRAYER

> Lord Jesus, I choose not to hold on to my resentment. I relinquish my right to seek revenge, and I ask You to heal my damaged emotions. Thank You for setting me free from the bondage of my bitterness. I now ask You to bless those who have hurt me. In Jesus' name I pray. Amen.

Resentments Toward God

Before we came to Christ, thoughts were raised up in our minds against a true knowledge of God (2 Corinthians 10:3-5). Even as believers we have harbored resentments toward God that will hinder our walk with Him. We should have a healthy fear of God (awe of His holiness, power, and presence), but we fear no punishment from Him. Romans 8:15 (NASB) reads, "For you have not received a spirit of slavery leading to fear again, but you have received a spirit of adoption as sons by which we cry out, 'Abba! Father!'"

The following exercise will help renew your mind to a true knowledge of your heavenly Father. Read the left column out loud and then read the corresponding right column. Begin each one with the statement in bold at the top of that list.

ACKNOWLEDGING THE TRUTH ABOUT YOUR FATHER GOD

I RENOUNCE THE LIE THAT GOD IS...	I CHOOSE TO BELIEVE THE TRUTH THAT GOD IS...
distant and disinterested.	intimate and involved [Psalm 139:1-18].
insensitive and uncaring.	kind and compassionate [Psalm 103:8-14].
stern and demanding.	accepting and filled with joy and love [Zephaniah 3:17; Romans 15:7].
passive and cold.	warm and affectionate [Isaiah 40:11; Hosea 11:3-4].
absent or too busy for me.	always with me and eager to be with me [see Jeremiah 31:20; Ezekiel 34:11-16; Hebrews 13:5].

never satisfied with what I do; impatient or angry.	patient and slow to anger [see Exodus 34:6; 2 Peter 3:9].
mean, cruel, or abusive.	loving, gentle, and protective of me [Psalm 18:2; Jeremiah 31:3; Isaiah 42:3].
trying to take all the fun out of life.	trustworthy, wanting to give me a full life. His will is good, perfect and acceptable for me [Lamentations 3:22-23; John 10:10; Romans 12:1-2].
controlling or manipulative.	full of grace and mercy; He gives me freedom to fail [Hebrews 4:15-16; Luke 15:11-16].
condemning or unforgiving.	tenderhearted and forgiving; His heart and arms are always open to me [Psalm 130:1-4; Luke 15:17-24].
nitpicking, exacting, or perfectionistic.	committed to my growth and proud of me as His beloved child [Romans 8:28-29; Hebrews 12:5-11; 2 Corinthians 7:4].

I am the apple of His eye! [See Deuteronomy 32:10.]

16

STEP 4:
REBELLION VS. SUBMISSION

We live in rebellious times. Many people sit in judgment of those in authority over them, and they submit only when it is convenient or because they are afraid of being caught. The Bible instructs us to pray for those in authority over us (1 Timothy 2:1-2) and submit to governing authorities (Romans 13:1-7). Rebelling against God and His established authority leaves us spiritually vulnerable. God permits us to disobey earthly leaders only when they require us to do something morally wrong or attempt to rule outside the realm of their authority. To have a submissive spirit and servant's heart, pray this prayer aloud.

PRAYER

> Dear heavenly Father, You have said that rebellion is as the sin of witchcraft and insubordination is as iniquity and idolatry [1 Samuel 15:23]. I know that I have not always been submissive, but instead have rebelled in my heart against You, and against those You have placed in authority over me, in attitude and in action. Please show me all the ways I have been rebellious. I choose now to adopt a submissive spirit and a servant's heart. In Jesus' name I pray. Amen.

It is an act of faith to trust God to work in our lives through less than perfect leaders, but that is what God is asking us to do. Should those in positions of leadership or power abuse their authority and break the laws designed to protect innocent people, you need to seek help from a higher authority. Many states require certain types of abuse to be reported to a governmental agency. If that is your situation, we urge you to get the help you need immediately.

But don't assume someone in authority is violating God's Word just because he or she is telling you to do something you don't like. God has set up specific lines of authority to protect us and give order to society. We respect the position of authority regardless of the person in that position. Without governing authorities, every society would be chaos. In the list below, allow the Lord to show you any specific ways you have been rebellious, and use the following prayer to confess those sins He brings to mind.

- ☐ civil government (including traffic laws, tax laws, attitude toward government officials) (Romans 13:1-7; 1 Timothy 2:1-4; 1 Peter 2:13-17)

- ☐ parents, stepparents, or legal guardians (Ephesians 6:1-3)

- ☐ teachers, coaches, school officials (Romans 13:1-4)

- ☐ employers (past and present) (1 Peter 2:18-23)

- ☐ husband (1 Peter 3:1-4) or wife (Ephesians 5:21; 1 Peter 3:7)

  [Husbands, ask the Lord if your lack of love for your wife could be fostering a rebellious spirit within her. If so, confess that as a violation of Ephesians 5:22-33.]

- ☐ church leaders (Hebrews 13:7)

- ☐ God (Daniel 9:5,9)

As the Spirit of God brings to your mind ways that you have been rebellious, use the following prayer to specifically confess each one.

PRAYER

Lord Jesus, I confess that I have been rebellious toward [name or position] by [specifically confess what you did or did not do]. Thank You for Your forgiveness. I choose to be submissive and obedient to Your Word. In Jesus' name I pray. Amen.

17

STEP 5:
PRIDE VS. HUMILITY

Pride comes before a fall, but God gives grace to the humble (James 4:6; 1 Peter 5:1-10). Humility is confidence properly placed in God, and we are instructed to "put no confidence in the flesh" (Philippians 3:3). We are to be "strong in the Lord and in the strength of His might" (Ephesians 6:10). Proverbs 3:5 urges us to trust in the Lord with all our hearts and not to lean on our own understanding. Use the following prayer to ask God to show you where you may be prideful.

PRAYER

Dear heavenly Father, You have said that pride goes before destruction and an arrogant spirit before stumbling. I confess that I have focused on my own needs and desires and not others'. I have not always denied myself, picked up my cross daily, and followed You. I have relied on my own strength and resources instead of resting in Yours. I have placed my will before Yours and centered my life around myself instead of You.

I confess my pride and selfishness and pray that all ground gained in my life by the enemies of the Lord Jesus Christ would be canceled. I choose to rely upon the Holy Spirit's power and guidance so that I will do nothing from selfishness or empty conceit. With humility of mind, I choose to regard others as more important than myself. I acknowledge You as my Lord and confess that apart from You I can do nothing of lasting significance. Please examine my heart and show me the specific ways I have lived my life in pride. In the gentle and humble name of Jesus I pray. Amen. [See Proverbs 16:18; Matthew 6:33; 16:24; Romans 12:10; Philippians 2:3.]

Pray through the list below and use the prayer following to confess any sins of pride the Lord brings to mind.

- ☐ having a stronger desire to do my will than God's will
- ☐ leaning too much on my own understanding and experience rather than seeking God's guidance through prayer and His Word
- ☐ relying on my own strengths and resources instead of depending on the power of the Holy Spirit
- ☐ being more concerned about controlling others than about developing self-control
- ☐ being too busy doing selfish and supposedly important things rather than seeking and doing God's will
- ☐ having a tendency to think I have no needs
- ☐ finding it hard to admit when I am wrong
- ☐ being more concerned about pleasing people than about pleasing God
- ☐ being overly concerned about getting the credit I feel I deserve
- ☐ thinking I am more humble, spiritual, religious, or devoted than others
- ☐ being driven to obtain recognition by attaining degrees, titles, and positions
- ☐ often feeling that my needs are more important than another person's needs
- ☐ considering myself better than others because of my academic, artistic, or athletic abilities and accomplishments
- ☐ not waiting on God
- ☐ other ways I have thought more highly of myself than I should

For each of the above areas that has been true in your life, pray this prayer aloud.

PRAYER

> Lord Jesus, I agree I have been proud by [name what you checked above]. Thank You for Your forgiveness. I choose to humble myself before You and others. I choose to place all my confidence in You and put no confidence in my flesh. In Jesus' name I pray. Amen.

18

STEP 6:
BONDAGE VS. FREEDOM

Many times we feel trapped in a vicious cycle that never seems to end: sin, confess, sin, confess, sin, confess…We can become very discouraged and just give up and give in to the sins of the flesh. In order to experience our freedom, we must follow James 4:7 (NASB): "Submit therefore to God. Resist the devil and he will flee from you." We submit to God by confession of sin and repentance (turning away from sin). We resist the devil by rejecting his lies. We must walk in the truth and put on the full armor of God (see Ephesians 6:10-18).

When a sin becomes a habit, breaking free often requires help from a trusted brother or sister in Christ. James 5:16 (NASB) says, "Confess your sins to one another, and pray for one another so that you may be healed. The effective prayer of a righteous man can accomplish much." For many people, the assurance of 1 John 1:9 NASB is enough: "If we confess our sins, He is faithful and righteous to forgive us our sins and to cleanse us from all unrighteousness."

Remember, confession is not saying, "I'm sorry." It is openly admitting, "I did it." Whether you need help from other people or just the accountability of walking in the light before God, pray this prayer aloud.

PRAYER

Dear heavenly Father, You have told me to put on the Lord Jesus Christ and make no provision for the flesh in regard to its lust. I confess that I have given in to fleshly lusts that wage war against my soul. I thank You that in Christ my sins are already forgiven, but I have broken Your holy law, and I have allowed sin to wage war in my body. I come to You now to confess and renounce these sins of the flesh so that I might be cleansed and set free from the bondage of sin. Please reveal to my mind all the sins of the flesh I have committed and the ways I have grieved the Holy Spirit. In Jesus' holy name I pray. Amen. [See Romans 6:12-13; 13:14; 2 Corinthians 4:2; James 4:1; 1 Peter 2:11; 5:8.]

The following list contains many sins of the flesh, but a prayerful examination of Mark 7:20-23; Galatians 5:19-21; Ephesians 4:25-31 and other Scripture passages will help you to be thorough. Look over those passages and the list below and ask the Holy Spirit to bring to your mind the sins you need to confess. He may reveal others to you as well. For each one the Lord shows you, pray a prayer of confession from your heart. There is a sample prayer following the list. (Sexual sins, eating disorders, substance abuse, abortion, suicidal tendencies, and perfectionism will be dealt with later in this step. Further counseling help may be necessary to find complete healing and freedom in these and other areas.)

- ☐ stealing
- ☐ quarreling/fighting
- ☐ jealousy/envy
- ☐ complaining/criticism
- ☐ sarcasm
- ☐ lustful actions

- ☐ gossip/slander
- ☐ swearing
- ☐ apathy/laziness
- ☐ lying
- ☐ hatred
- ☐ anger
- ☐ lustful thoughts

- ☐ drunkenness
- ☐ cheating
- ☐ procrastination
- ☐ greed/materialism
- ☐ others:

PRAYER

Lord Jesus, I confess that I have sinned against You by [name the sins]. Thank You for Your forgiveness and cleansing. I now turn away from these expressions of sin and turn to You, Lord. Fill me with Your Holy Spirit so that I will not carry out the desires of the flesh. In Jesus' name I pray. Amen.

If you are struggling with habitual sin, read *Overcoming Addictive Behavior* (Regal Books, 2003) and *Winning the Battle Within* (Harvest House, 2004).

Resolving Sexual Sin

We are responsible to not let sin reign (rule) in our mortal bodies. We must not use our bodies or other people's bodies as instruments of unrighteousness (see Romans 6:12-13). Sexual immorality is not only a sin against God but also a sin against our bodies, which are temples of the Holy Spirit (1 Corinthians 6:18-19). To find freedom from sexual bondage, begin by praying this prayer.

PRAYER

> Lord Jesus, I have allowed sin to reign in my mortal body. I ask You to bring to my mind every sexual use of my body as an instrument of unrighteousness so I can renounce the sexual sins and break the sinful bondages. In Jesus' name I pray. Amen.

As the Lord brings to your mind every immoral sexual use of your body, whether it was done to you (rape, incest, sexual molestation) or willingly by you (pornography, masturbation, sexual immorality), use this prayer to renounce *every* experience you can think of.

PRAYER

> Lord Jesus, I renounce [name the sexual experience] with [name]. I ask You to break that sinful bond with [name] spiritually, physically, and emotionally.

After you are finished, commit your body to the Lord with this prayer.

PRAYER

> Lord Jesus, I renounce all these uses of my body as an instrument of unrighteousness, and I admit to any willful participation. I choose to present my physical body to You as an instrument of righteousness, a living and holy sacrifice, acceptable to You. I choose to reserve the sexual use of my body for marriage only. I reject the devil's lie that my body is not clean or that it is dirty or in any way unacceptable to You as a result of my past sexual experiences. Lord, thank You that You have cleansed and forgiven me and that You love and accept me just the way I am. Therefore, I choose now to accept myself and my body as clean in Your eyes. In Jesus' name I pray. Amen.

Pornography

PRAYER

> Lord Jesus, I confess that I have looked at sexually suggestive and pornographic material for the purpose of stimulating myself sexually. I have attempted to satisfy my lustful desires and have polluted my body, soul, and spirit. Thank You for cleansing me and for Your forgiveness. I renounce any satanic bonds I have allowed in my life through the unrighteous use of my body and mind. Lord, I commit myself to destroy any objects in my possession that I have used for sexual stimulation, and I turn away from all media that are associated with my sexual sin. I commit myself to the renewing of my mind and to thinking pure thoughts. Fill me with your Holy Spirit that I may not carry out the desires of the flesh. In Jesus' name I pray. Amen.

Homosexuality

PRAYER

> Lord Jesus, I renounce the lie that You have created me or anyone else to be homosexual, and I agree that in Your Word, You clearly forbid homosexual behavior. I choose to accept myself as a child of God, and I thank You that You created me as a [man or woman]. I renounce all homosexual thoughts, urges, drives, and acts, and I renounce all the ways Satan has used these things to pervert my relationships. I announce that I am free in Christ to relate to the opposite sex and my own sex in the way that You intended. In Jesus' name I pray. Amen.

Abortion

PRAYER

> Lord Jesus, I confess that I was not a proper guardian and keeper of the life You entrusted to me, and I confess that I have sinned. Thank You that because of Your forgiveness, I can forgive myself. I commit the child to You for all eternity and believe that he or she is in Your caring hands. In Jesus' name I pray. Amen.

Suicidal Tendencies

PRAYER

> Lord Jesus, I renounce all suicidal thoughts and any attempts I've made to take my own life or in any way injure myself. I renounce the lie that life is hopeless and that I can find peace and freedom by taking my own life. Satan is a thief and comes to steal, kill, and destroy. I choose life in Christ, who said He came to give me life and give it abundantly. Thank You for Your forgiveness, which allows me to forgive myself. I choose to believe that there is always hope in Christ and that my heavenly Father loves me. In Jesus' name I pray. Amen.

Drivenness and Perfectionism

PRAYER

> Heavenly Father, I renounce the lie that my sense of worth depends on my ability to perform. I announce the truth that my identity and sense of worth are found in who I am as Your child. I renounce seeking the approval and acceptance of other people, and I choose to believe that I am already approved and accepted in Christ because

of His death and resurrection. I choose to believe the truth that I have been saved—not by deeds done in righteousness, but according to Your mercy. I choose to believe that I am no longer under the curse of the law because Christ became a curse for me. I receive the free gift of life in Christ and choose to abide in Him. I renounce striving for perfection by living under the law. By Your grace, heavenly Father, I choose from this day forward to walk by faith in the power of Your Holy Spirit according to what You have said is true. In Jesus' name I pray. Amen.

Eating Disorders or Self-Mutilation

PRAYER

Lord Jesus, I renounce the lie that my value as a person depends on my appearance or performance. I renounce cutting, abusing myself, vomiting, using laxatives, and starving myself as means of being in control, altering my appearance, or trying to cleanse myself of evil. I announce that only the blood of the Lord Jesus Christ cleanses me from sin. I realize that I have been bought with a price and that my body, the temple of the Holy Spirit, belongs to God. Therefore, I choose to glorify God in my body. I renounce the lie that I am evil or that any part of my body is evil. Thank You that You accept me just the way I am in Christ. In Jesus' name I pray. Amen.

Substance Abuse

PRAYER

Lord Jesus, I confess that I have misused substances [alcohol, tobacco, food, prescription or street drugs] for the purpose of pleasure, to escape reality, or to cope with difficult problems. I confess that I have abused my body and programmed my mind in harmful ways. I have quenched the Holy Spirit as well. Thank You for Your forgiveness. I renounce any satanic connection or influence in my life through my misuse of food or chemicals. I cast my anxieties onto Christ, who loves me. I commit myself to yield no longer to substance abuse, and I choose to allow the Holy Spirit to direct and empower me. In Jesus' name I pray. Amen.

STEP 7:
CURSES VS. BLESSINGS

Scripture declares that the iniquities of one generation can be visited on the third and fourth generations, but God's blessings will be poured out on thousands of generations of those who love and obey Him (Exodus 20:4-6). The iniquities of one generation can adversely affect future ones unless those sins are renounced and a new spiritual heritage in Christ is claimed. This cycle of abuse and all negative influences can be stopped through genuine repentance. Jesus died for our sins, but you appropriate the forgiveness and cleansing only when you choose to believe Him, and you experience it only when you repent. You are not guilty of your ancestors' sins, but you were affected by their influence. Jesus said that after we have been fully trained we will be like our teachers (Luke 6:40), and Peter wrote that you were redeemed from your futile way of life inherited from your forefathers (1 Peter 1:18). Ask the Lord to reveal your ancestral sins and then renounce them with this prayer.

PRAYER

> Dear heavenly Father, please reveal to my mind all the sins of my ancestors that have been passed down through family lines. Since I am a new creation in Christ, I want to experience my freedom from those influences and walk in my new identity as a child of God. In Jesus' name I pray. Amen.
>
> Lord, I renounce [confess all the family sins that God brings to your mind].

Satan and people may curse us, but no curse will have any effect on us unless we believe it. We cannot passively take our place in Christ; we must actively and intentionally choose to submit to God and resist the devil, and then he will flee from us. Complete this final step with this declaration and prayer.

DECLARATION

I here and now reject and disown all the sins of my ancestors. As one who has been delivered from the domain of darkness and transferred into the kingdom of God's Son, I declare myself to be free from those harmful influences. I am no longer in Adam. I am now alive in Christ. Therefore I am the recipient of the blessings of God on my life as I choose to love and obey Him. As one who has been crucified and raised with Christ and who sits with Him in heavenly places, I renounce any and all satanic attacks and assignments directed against me and my ministry. Every curse placed on me was broken when Christ became a curse for me by dying on the cross [Galatians 3:13]. I reject any and every way in which Satan may claim ownership of me.

I belong to the Lord Jesus Christ, who purchased me with His own precious blood. I declare myself to be fully and eternally signed over and committed to the Lord Jesus Christ. Therefore, having submitted to God and by His authority, I now resist the devil, and I command every spiritual enemy of the Lord Jesus Christ to leave my presence. I put on the armor of God, and I stand against Satan's temptations, accusations, and deceptions. From this day forward I will seek to do only the will of my heavenly Father.

PRAYER

Dear heavenly Father, I come to You as Your child, bought out of slavery to sin by the blood of the Lord Jesus Christ. You are the Lord of the universe and the Lord of my life. I submit my body to You as a living and holy sacrifice. May You be glorified through my life and body. I now ask You to fill me with Your Holy Spirit. I commit myself to the renewing of my mind in order that I may prove that Your will is good, acceptable, and perfect for me. I desire nothing more than to be like You. I pray, believe, and do all this in the wonderful name of Jesus, my Lord and Savior. Amen.

Maintaining Your Freedom

It is exciting to experience your freedom in Christ, but what you have gained must be maintained. You have won an important battle, but the war goes on. To maintain your freedom in Christ and grow in the grace of God, you must continue renewing your mind to the truth of God's Word. If you become aware of lies you have believed, renounce them and choose the truth. If more painful memories surface, forgive those who hurt you and renounce any sinful part you played. Many people choose to go through the Steps to Freedom again on their own to make sure they have dealt with all their issues. Sometimes new issues will surface. The process can assist you in a regular "house cleaning."

After going though the Steps, people commonly have thoughts like these: "Nothing has really changed. I'm the same person I always was. It didn't work." In most cases you should just ignore these thoughts. We are not called to dispel the darkness, but to turn on the light. You don't get rid of negative thoughts by rebuking every one; you get rid of them by repenting and choosing the truth.

I encourage you to read *Victory over the Darkness* (Regal Books, 2000) and *The Bondage Breaker* (Harvest House, 2007) if you haven't already done so. The 21-day devotional *Walking in Freedom* (Regal Books, 2009) was written for those who have gone through the Steps. If you would like to continue growing in the grace of God, here are my suggestions:

1. Get rid of or destroy any cult or occult objects in your home. (See Acts 19:18-20.)

2. Get involved in a small-group ministry where you can be a real person, and be part of a church where God's truth is taught with kindness and grace.

3. Read and meditate on the truth of God's Word each day.

4. Don't let your mind be passive, especially concerning what you watch and listen to (music, TV, movies, and the like). Actively take every thought captive to the obedience of Christ.

5. Learn to pray by the Spirit (see *Praying by the Power of the Spirit*, Harvest House, 2003).

6. Remember, you are responsible for your mental, spiritual, and physical health (for the latter, see *The Biblical Guide to Alternative Medicine*, Regal Books, 2003).

7. Work through *The Daily Discipler* (Regal Books, 2005) or *Daily in Christ* (Harvest House, 2000). The first is a practical systematic theology set in five daily readings per week for a year. The latter is a one-year devotional.

DAILY PRAYER AND DECLARATION

Dear heavenly Father, I praise You and honor You as my Lord and Savior. You are in control of all things. I thank You that You are always with me and will never leave me or forsake me. You are the all-powerful and only wise God. You are kind and loving in all Your ways. I love You and thank You that I am united with Christ and spiritually alive in Him. I choose not to love the world or the things in the world, and I crucify the flesh and all its passions.

Thank You for the life I now have in Christ. I ask You to fill me with the Holy Spirit so I can be guided by You and not carry out the desires of the flesh. I declare my total dependence upon You, and I take my stand against Satan and all his lying ways. I choose to believe the truth of God's Word despite what my feelings may say. I refuse to be discouraged; You are the God of all hope. Nothing is too difficult for You. I am confident that You will supply all my needs as I seek to live according to Your Word. I thank You that I can be content and live a responsible life through Christ who strengthens me.

I now take my stand against Satan and command him and all his evil spirits to depart from me. I choose to put on the full armor of God so I may be able to stand firm against all the devil's schemes. I submit my body as a living and holy sacrifice to You, and I choose to renew my mind by Your living Word. By so doing I will be able to prove that Your will is good, acceptable, and perfect for me. In the name of my Lord and Savior, Jesus Christ, I pray. Amen.

BEDTIME PRAYER

Thank You, Lord, that You have brought me into Your family and have blessed me with every spiritual blessing in the heavenly places in Christ Jesus. Thank You for this time of renewal and refreshment through sleep. I accept it as one of Your blessings for Your children, and I trust You to guard my mind and my body during my sleep.

As I have thought about You and Your truth during the day, I choose to let those good thoughts continue in my mind while I am asleep. I commit myself to You for Your protection against every attempt of Satan and his demons to attack me during sleep. Guard my mind from nightmares. I renounce all fear and cast every anxiety upon You, Lord. I commit myself to You as my rock, my fortress, and my strong tower. May Your peace be upon this place of rest. In the strong name of the Lord Jesus Christ I pray. Amen.

PRAYER FOR SPIRITUALLY CLEANSING A HOME, APARTMENT, OR ROOM

After removing and destroying all objects of false worship, pray this prayer aloud in every room:

Heavenly Father, I acknowledge that You are the Lord of heaven and earth. In Your sovereign power and love, You have entrusted me with many things. Thank You for this place to live. I claim my home as a place of spiritual safety for me and my family, and I ask for Your protection from all the attacks of the enemy. As a child of God, raised up and seated with Christ in the heavenly places, I command every evil spirit claiming ground in this place—based on the activities of past or present occupants, including me and my family—to leave and never return. I renounce all demonic assignments directed against this place. I ask You, heavenly Father, to post Your holy angels around this place to guard it from any and all attempts of the enemy to enter and disturb Your purposes for me and my family. I thank You, Lord, for doing this in the name of the Lord Jesus Christ. Amen.

PRAYER FOR LIVING IN A NON-CHRISTIAN ENVIRONMENT

After removing and destroying all objects of false worship from your possession, pray this aloud in the place where you live.

Thank You, heavenly Father, for a place to live and to be renewed by sleep. I ask You to set aside my room as a place of spiritual safety for me. I renounce any allegiance given to false gods or spirits by other occupants. I renounce any claim to this room by Satan based on the activities of past or present occupants, including me. On the basis of my position as a child of God and joint heir with Christ, who has all authority in heaven and on earth, I command all evil spirits to leave this place and never return. I ask You, heavenly Father, to station Your holy angels to protect me while I live here. In Jesus' mighty name I pray. Amen.

Paul prays in Ephesians 1:18-19 (NASB), "I pray that the eyes of your heart may be enlightened, so that you will know what is the hope of His calling, what are the riches of the glory of His inheritance in the saints, and what is the surpassing greatness of His power toward us who believe." Beloved, you are a child of God (1 John 3:1), and "my God will supply all your needs according to His riches in glory in Christ Jesus" (Philippians 4:19 NASB). The critical needs are the "being" needs, such as eternal or spiritual life, which He has given you, and an identity, which you have in Christ. In addition, Jesus has met your needs for acceptance, security, and significance. Memorize and meditate on the following truths daily from the devotional *Who I Am in Christ* (Regal Books, 2001). Read the entire list aloud morning and evening for the next few weeks. Think about what you are reading and let the truth of who you are in Christ renew your mind. This is your inheritance in Christ.

IN CHRIST

I renounce the lie that I am rejected, unloved, or shameful. In Christ I am *accepted*. God says...

I am God's child (John 1:12).

I am Christ's friend (John 15:5).

I have been justified (Romans 5:1).

I am united with the Lord, and I am one spirit with Him (1 Corinthians 6:17).

I have been bought with a price, so I belong to God (1 Corinthians 6:19-20).

I am a member of Christ's body (1 Corinthians 12:27).

I am a saint, a holy one (Ephesians 1:1).

I have been adopted as God's child (Ephesians 1:5).

I have direct access to God through the Holy Spirit (Ephesians 2:18).

I have been redeemed and forgiven of all my sins (Colossians 1:14).

I am complete in Christ (Colossians 2:10).

I renounce the lie that I am guilty, unprotected, alone, or abandoned. In Christ I am *secure*. God says...

I am free from condemnation (Romans 8:1-2).

I am assured that God will work all things together for my good (Romans 8:28).

I am free from any condemning charges against me (Romans 8:31-34).

I cannot be separated from the love of God (Romans 8:35-39).

I have been established, anointed, and sealed by God (2 Corinthians 1:21-22).

I am confident that the good work God has begun in me will be perfected (Philippians 1:6).

I am a citizen of heaven (Philippians 3:20).

I am hidden with Christ in God (Colossians 3:3).

I have not been given a spirit of fear, but of power, love, and discipline (2 Timothy 1:7).

I can find grace and mercy to help in time of need (Hebrews 4:16).

I am born of God, and the evil one cannot touch me (1 John 5:18).

I renounce the lie that I am worthless, inadequate, helpless, or hopeless. In Christ I am *significant*. God says...

I am the salt of the earth and the light of the world (Matthew 5:13-14).

I am a branch of the true vine, Jesus, and a channel of His life (John 15:1,5).

I have been chosen and appointed by God to bear fruit (John 15:16).

I am a personal, Spirit-empowered witness of Christ's (Acts 1:8).

I am a temple of God (1 Corinthians 3:16).

I am a minister of reconciliation for God (2 Corinthians 5:17-21).

I am God's coworker (2 Corinthians 6:1).

I am seated with Christ in the heavenly realm (Ephesians 2:6).

I am God's workmanship, created for good works (Ephesians 2:10).

I may approach God with freedom and confidence (Ephesians 3:12).

I can do all things through Christ who strengthens me! (Philippians 4:13).

I am not the great I AM,
but by the grace of God I am what I am.
(See Exodus 3:14; John 8:24,28,58; 1 Corinthians 15:10.)

More Great Harvest House Products
by Neil Anderson

The Bondage Breaker®

Walk away from the shadows and shackles in your life and enjoy the freedom of knowing who you are in Christ. Neil helps you break negative thought patterns, control irrational feelings, and break out of the bondage of sinful behavior. Also available…

The Bondage Breaker® Study Guide
The Bondage Breaker™ DVD Experience
The Bondage Breaker®—the Next Step
The Bondage Breaker® Youth Edition

The Core of Christianity

Neil addresses four tendencies that mislead Christians—legalism, liberalism, spiritism, and false prophets—and offers clear, biblical paths you can follow to overcome them.

Winning the Battle Within

Has God's wonderful gift of sex become an area of spiritual slavery for you? You can turn from a distorted view of sex, let go of guilt and shame, and overcome sexual struggles with practical steps based on God's Word. (Formerly titled *Finding Freedom In a Sex-Obsessed World*.)

Breaking the Bondage of Legalism

Here's encouragement for you when you feel defeated. Neil Anderson, Rich Miller, and Paul Travis expose the trauma of legalism—shame, guilt, pride—and show how knowing who you are in Christ liberates you from trying to be "good enough for God."

Praying by the Power of the Spirit

How can you intimately connect with God? Find out about your freedom to be honest with your Father; release from bondage through prayer; and how God leads you to love *Him*, not His blessings. Includes study questions.

Getting Anger Under Control

Whether horrific enough to grab headlines or minor enough to cause arguments with family and friends, uncontrolled anger steals peace, joy, and trust. Here are clear, biblical methods for keeping anger in its place.

Daily in Christ

Tired of trying to live the Christian life in your own strength? This 365-day devotional is a refreshing invitation to live in Christ and be refreshed by the Father's love.

Freedom from Fear

What are the root causes of fear? How do strongholds develop? How can you tear down the prison walls? Find out in this 360-page book, which includes a 21-day devotional guide.

Winning Spiritual Warfare

This 48-page pocket-size book contains selections from *The Bondage Breaker*. For every lie that holds you captive, there is truth that will set you free. Discover the concrete steps you can take to overcome the bondage of spiritual strongholds and win the battle for your mind.

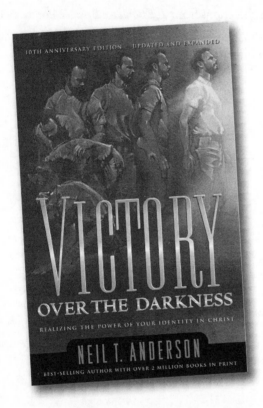